Guy —
Best regards —
Andrew R.
Thornburg

Million Dollar
NETWORKING

ALSO BY ANDREA R. NIERENBERG

Nonstop Networking: How to Improve Your Life, Luck, and Career

Save 25% when you order any Capital title from our Web site: www.capital-books.com.

The Sure Way to Find, Grow, and Keep Your Business

Andrea R. Nierenberg

Million Dollar
NETWORKING

CAPITAL BOOKS, INC.
STERLING, VIRGINIA

Capital Books, Inc.

P.O. Box 605

Herndon, Virginia 20172-0605

ISBN 1-933102-05-5   (alk. paper)

Library of Congress Cataloging-in-Publication Data

Nierenberg, Andrea R.

  Million dollar networking : the sure way to find, grow, and keep your business : capital ideas for business & personal development / Andrea Nierenberg.-- 1st ed.

     p. cm.

  Includes bibliographical references and index.

  ISBN 1-933102-05-5 (cloth)

  1. Business networks. I. Title.

  HD69.S8N53 2005

  650.1'3--dc22   2005009353

Printed in the United States of America on acid-free paper that meets the American National Standards Institute Z39-48 Standard.

First Edition

10 9 8 7 6 5 4 3 2 1

DEDICATION

To my wonderful parents, who always taught me life's greatest lessons.

To my dear mother, Molly—thank you for your continuing support, encouragement, and love. You are truly the best!

To my dear father, Paul—I think of you always and know you are continuing to spread good cheer and terrific advice to all of those you are meeting in heaven. I know that you are always looking down and smiling at me. And yes, Daddy, I continue to give everyone I meet "a smile and a handshake!"

CONTENTS

ACKNOWLEDGMENTS

When my great publisher, Kathleen Hughes, asked me, "How about a second book?" I thought that it would be wonderful to do it, especially because I had compiled a lot more information, material, and examples for the business community since writing *Nonstop Networking*. Then I sat back and wondered, "How will I do it all?"

There are so many of you in my life whom I want to thank, and I hope you know who you are. I wish there was enough paper to list everyone.

Those I first want to acknowledge and thank are the people who helped me turn my thoughts, words, and stories into a simple and easy-to-read guide on finding, growing, and keeping your business relationships.

To Tom Ciesielka for continuing to be my head cheerleader and balance beam as the wonderful publicist and marketer he has been to me for the last nine years. Tom has an amazing team working with him, and they have also been the lifeblood of this book: Duane Sherman, an amazing editor and my favorite "process" person—he really combed and edited through each chapter and made each one come to life; Ian North, a bright and rising star who has diligently captured "my voice" and has great organizational skills; and Margaret Larkin, who is my favorite introvert! Margaret has helped with both this book and my first one, and has taught me a lot through the way she looks at information. To the whole team at TC Public Relations—again, a "million dollar" thank you!

A big thanks to Kathleen Hughes, Publisher of Capital Books, and to Jane Graf and Jennifer Hughes for your continued belief in me. I look forward to our next exciting journey together.

I was with a colleague and friend from the direct marketing industry, Diane Silverman, in my office, talking over a cup of tea about a good name for this book, when she said, "How about 'Million Dollar Networking'?" So, Diane, thank you for coming up with the catchy title.

I am blessed to have so many friends, colleagues, mentors, and partners in my life and work. I want to thank all of my clients and the participants from my workshops and speaking engagements who have helped me fine tune and build on the models we have created and discussed.

To Jon Lambert, whose wit, humor, insight, brilliance, and friendship will always hold a special place in my heart.

To Lois Geller, my best pal, whose friendship, creativity, and laugh always put a smile on my face. She has been through a challenging year and her amazing spirit continues to pull her through.

To Helen Ray Budelli, who has been a great assistant and organizational consultant, and who has helped me totally become even more organized than I ever thought I was!

This book could never have come to life without the many energies and perspectives of the many great people I know who have touched my life. It is impossible to name everyone because I have been touched by so many incredible people.

The following people stand out in their help and support of me during the writing of this book: Arlene Adler, Vicky Amon, Max Bartko, Jim Blasingame, Anita Brick, Andrew Carr, Judith Cavaliere, Denise Clancey, Vanessa Cognard, Ross Dabrow, Bruce Dorskind, Karen Duncan, Dave Ehlers, Mike Faulkner, Susie Greewood, Gail Goodman, Bill Gunn, Steven James, Judy and Ken Karpinski, Margie Kraker, Dan Kisch, Lynn Leffert, Allan Miller, Susan Miller, Bill O'Leary, Melissa Pordy, Rick Miners, Trudy and Bill Mitchell, Elaine Pofeldt, Nick Risom, Gregg Robbins, Norma Rosenberg,

Paul Schaye, Jeri Sedlar, Lisa Merizio Smith, Mike Spring, Sharon Sullivan, Bill Squiteri, Scott Swedenburg, Steve Topper, and Bill Wreaks.

Thank you to my brother, Richard, and my sister, Meredith, for their love and encouragement, and of course to my wonderful mother, Molly, who always believes in me and never fails to always tell it like it is! For those of you who know her, you would certainly agree! And to my loving father Paul, who was my hero. I know he continually looks down from heaven with that adorable grin that lights up any room, and I'm sure it's continuing to light up heaven!

INTRODUCTION

"May I have your card?" I asked Sabrina, a woman I met recently at a birthday party. She had told me she was in real estate, a business where everyone is constantly "networking" for new clients, and I offered to send her a copy of my first book, *Nonstop Networking*.

She didn't have her card with her, yet she did tell me her name and where she worked. At the end of the evening, we said goodbye, and I'm sure she thought I'd forget to send the book since she couldn't give me her card. Even though I didn't have it, I wrote down her name and company on my notepad (an important networking tool). The next morning, I called her company, found out she worked in the main office (they have eight branch offices), and sent her a copy.

Three days later, she called me and said, "Thank you. I'm blown away for three reasons." What were they?

1. I remembered her name and her company (I wrote it down).

2. I found out her company address (I was resourceful).

3. I sent her the book (I actually followed through).

She was so impressed, she told me, that she was going to give the book to Steve, the vice president of sales, with the hope that he might invite me to speak with the other brokers in her firm. A week later, Steve called me and invited me to speak about networking to two hundred brokers. Some days before I was scheduled to give my presentation, I sent an email to Sabrina (her preferred method of communication) to thank her (she was my original contact).

When I arrived at the workshop site, I looked around the large room and saw three people I recognized. One was a neighbor from my building. We had always smiled and said hello, but never formally met. Now Bernie and I are friends, as well as working colleagues, and I always refer her to others who are looking for a real estate agent. I recognized another woman from my health club. Since then, when we see each other in class, we always greet each other warmly. The third person was someone I had seen in a store speaking rudely to one of the salespeople. Needless to say, I would be hesitant to refer her to any of my clients. We all have bad days, but in the world of business networking and in life, the golden rule always applies.

So, because of that chance meeting at the birthday party, and because I took the opportunity to follow up, was resourceful, and thanked my networking contacts in the firm, I got the job and I am now scheduled to speak to all eight branches of this large real estate firm.

It all began when I went to the party prepared with my:

- networking tool kit,
- "networking awareness" primed, and
- system for follow-up and follow-through in place.

By the way, in case you are wondering, I immediately went back and thanked my friend, Bruce, the host of the birthday party, and have kept him posted about my success with the real estate firm. I've also continued to thank Sabrina and Steve every time I'm referred to another office. Why? Because they were the first to recommend my services.

I make it a practice before any engagement to say thank you to all of the people who've referred me, which is part of my "Thank-You Chain" (more about that later). And I always thank them by their preferred method—some like email, others prefer voice mail.

Ever since I wrote *Nonstop Networking*, I have seen over and over how personal contacts can turn into professional ones. In fact, the art of

effective networking is absolutely vital to building solid business relationships and to finding, growing, and keeping your business.

To make sure that this book covers everything businesspeople
need to know, I asked some of my business clients to share their questions
about networking. Here's what they asked and what we discuss fully in
Million Dollar Networking:

- How do I start a conversation with someone I find intimidating?
- How do I ask tough questions tactfully?
- How do I start and exit a conversation at internal and external
  business events?
- How do I "network" with someone I may not like, but who is
  key in the department or industry?
- What are some of the topics to avoid?
- What are examples of great opening lines, icebreakers, and
  small talk when I'm networking?
- How do I follow up?
- How do I establish and create advocates and referral opportunities?
- How do I know when I'm networking?
- Where can I find a systematic approach to networking?
- How can I keep all of my contacts organized and easy to reach?
- How can I continue to find, grow, and keep my business all the time?
- How do I develop my own "self-brand"?

These are the kinds of questions thousands of businesspeople
from around the globe have been asking me for the past fifteen years.
Thus the subtitle of this book—*The Sure Way to Find, Grow, and Keep
Your Business*—comes directly from my Find! Grow! Keep! Business
Development System©. This is really what networking is all about; and this,
we hope, is what you will take away with you.

For those who are seasoned professionals, some of what you'll find in *Million Dollar Networking* will be a refresher course, a checklist for following up, and a guide to new techniques for building your network and keeping it growing. For those new to the strategies of reaching out to your personal and professional contacts and making them part of your business plan, you will find concrete tools for tapping your social skills, becoming a resource for others, and building a network that can help your business and profession.

Many of us already know why we need to network constantly. Unfortunately, the word has been misunderstood and has a negative image because so many people are only interested in "what's in it for me" and want quick results. I've made it my goal in business to teach that networking is the process of developing and maintaining quality relationships that enrich our lives and empower us to achieve our goals. It's about giving first and realizing that we can learn from everyone we meet.

What we now need is a step-by-step approach to network effectively and methodically and to fit it into our everyday life, no matter who we are or what we do. We must also practice networking consistently. Someone in a training session once told me that networking is similar to flossing your teeth—if you fail to do it every day, you won't reap the benefits.

Million Dollar Networking is about how to increase your business and achieve your goals—by reaching out to people. You will learn and be reminded of a simple system that is easy to remember and easy to implement and is based on five simple steps:

1. Meet new people and nurture your current network.

2. Listen and learn from everyone with whom you connect.

3. Make quality connections for others.

4. Follow up.

5. Stay in touch creatively.

You will see how networking is a lifelong process and a state of mind. The opposite of "networking" is "not working." Ross, a client who's become a friend, told me that many business professionals understand how to provide their clients with excellent customer service during the "state of the transaction." The challenge is learning how to maintain and cultivate that same relationship between transactions.

How do you distinguish yourself from others, move your business relationships to the next level, and also be time sensitive and efficient? One goal, as Ross told me, is to find a way to leverage relationships into "dynamic partnerships." Each part of finding, growing, and keeping business relationships weaves into another, and you have to have all three components to create really strong business and personal relationships that will help your business.

You might be wondering who should network. The answer, of course, is that everyone should, especially if you are interested in having more clients, building more business, and feeling more in control of your future. Ask yourself:

- Who am I? Am I an entrepreneur, part of a small or large company, a manager or salesperson?
- What are my goals, and how do I wish to achieve them?
- What do I have to offer others?
- What can I give, and how can I be a resource?
- How do I market myself with my experience and expertise?
- Where and when will I do it—everywhere and all the time?

Million Dollar Networking is divided into three parts. In Part 1 you'll discover how to *find* new connections. Part 2 shows you how to *grow* your relationships with those clients to their fullest potential, and in Part 3 you'll learn how to *keep* your clients coming back. Each chapter is illustrated with success stories from my personal experience and the experiences of those with whom I've worked. Each chapter concludes with exercises you can do over and over as you build on the skills you've learned.

We all have the tools inside of us—it's just a matter of developing a system and sticking to it. Or, as Charles Schulz so aptly said, "Life is like a ten-speed bike. Most of us have gears we never use."

So here we go together. I hope you enjoy the journey as much as I enjoyed writing and learning from all of this. Remember Dr. Norman Vincent Peale's unforgettable words: "Formulate and stamp indelibly on your mind a mental picture of yourself as succeeding. Hold this picture tenaciously and never permit it to fade. Your mind will seek to develop this picture."

PART I
FIND:
Meeting People

"The heart of the discerning acquires knowledge;
the ears of the wise seek it out."
—Proverbs 18:15

Whatever we do, it is important to get business and find relationships that will continue throughout our lives. In order to "find," we must also have a strategy, plan, and tactics to put into place that will help us every day. Although some people may consider themselves the "hunters," or the ones who find new opportunities, we need to see how each and every one of us in business can fine-tune our skills as we create new relationships and build and nurture the ones we have.

In the first section of this book, we tackle only those aspects involved in finding relationships and business opportunities—everything from meeting new people to where and how you do it easily and efficiently. You'll learn what to do at an "event" to make your time more efficient and productive as you are networking. I have also put together a model that you can add to and modify according to your needs.

CHAPTER

Who Do You Know?

> *"The ladder of success is best climbed by stepping on the rungs of opportunity."*—**Ayn Rand**

Sitting on an airplane one day awaiting takeoff, I looked around the cabin and realized that each person had his or her own story, life, and many different networks. Any conversation could teach me something new or let me help the person I talked with.

I decided to experiment and noticed that the woman sitting across the aisle was reading a book on sales and marketing. When we were served our sodas and nuts, I asked her if the book was interesting and mentioned that I hadn't read that one yet. We began our conversation, and I learned that she was a new sales manager for a software company and was on her way to a sales meeting in Los Angeles. Through some open-ended, conversational questions I asked, I learned the following:

- She lived in New York City, in the same building as a friend of mine, and they knew each other.
- She formerly worked for a company where I had presented a workshop.
- She was an active alumni member of a college that my friend's daughter was interested in and said she would write a letter of recommendation to the admissions office.

What I realized through this exchange was that in business networking happens anywhere, anytime; and you never know how starting a conversation with someone can open doors and opportunities for both parties involved. Woody Allen, in a recent movie, has one of his characters say, "Networking is life."

The art of networking, which I define as the combination of people skills, interaction, and opportunity, is an absolutely vital tool for building business and keeping it. Networking is about creating and developing opportunities through meeting and "connecting the dots" among the people you know. Over time, as you build rapport and trust, these relationships lead to other contacts, relationships, and opportunities.

Through this amazing linking of trusted advisors, friends, and advocates, the power created is stunning. Think of those you know who are truly masterful at networking and ask yourself: How do they do it, and what do they do? You will also find that the "best practices" vary greatly. No matter what their style, these people all know and have confidence and respect for each other.

Now think of all the networks you already have:

- Jobs
- Social activities
- Religious affiliations
- Neighborhoods
- Clubs
- Business associations
- School alumni

The list could go on and on.

I read in a great book that we all know at least 250 people. Look at the group of people you know who fit on this list and you'll discover how to multiply your network when you realize that you can help many

THE POST OFFICE—AT THE FRONT OF THE LINE

Reaching the front of the line, I began talking with the clerk, to whom I had given a copy of my first book. While we talked, I found out that he liked the book so much, he was going to recommend to upper management that copies of it be bought for post offices throughout New York.

THE COFFEE SHOP

While sipping an espresso, I was talking with a friend about his advertising business. Noticing that the man at the next table was listening, I introduced myself and asked if he was in advertising as well. He said he was, but he was currently looking for a job. I introduced the two men and later heard that the man at the next table got an interview at my friend's business.

These examples show that almost any person you come in contact with could be a potential networking contact. Be aware and develop new business opportunities when you're:

- on an airplane,
- at the dentist's office,
- waiting in line for movie tickets,
- even at the drycleaner.

Got another example? Network with me at info@mybusinessrelationships.com.

of these people, who in turn can connect you with some of the 250 people each of them knows. In my own life this number has multiplied many times over!

By the way, the woman from the plane and I have stayed in touch. She was able to help my friend's daughter get into the college she wanted (she also did have great grades and was an athlete and an all-around terrific young lady, yet my new friend's influence did help).

I have done several workshops for her new company, and I also went back to her former company, which is a client, and reconnected with them. By building with our mutual friend there, I made more incredible connections that led to great business relationships that I am still nurturing today.

Here is one reason I hope you're reading this book: to learn to look at life with a networking eye and ear and realize that opportunities can unfold anywhere, anytime. You just have to be ready, willing, able, and open to starting some conversations.

Right now, write down the names of up to three people you know in each of the following categories:

Job/workplace: _____

_____

_____

Social activities: _____

_____

_____

Religious affiliations: _____

_____

_____

Neighborhood: _____

_____

_____

Clubs: _____

_____

_____

Professional associations: _____

_____

_____

School/alumni associations: _____

_____

_____

Now look over these names and recall how you met some of these people. How were you introduced? Did you introduce them to others? I'd like you to dig down here and perhaps jog your memory. What I'm doing is allowing you to reach back and realize that networking has been part of your life, even if you never thought about it consciously.

Part of growing and strengthening our business networks is remembering how and who else was involved when we met and realizing that each of us probably does know more than 250 people!

People You Need in Your Network

The first step in building a network is to identify the people with whom you want to build relationships. You will be pleasantly surprised at how many of them you already know. The types of people you need in your network most likely include:

1. Customers or clients

2. Suppliers

3. Co-workers and colleagues

4. People in your profession

5. People you went to school with or met at a seminar or workshop

6. Like-minded people

7. Neighbors

8. Friends

9. Family

10. People you meet "in everyday life"

Customers or Clients

These people are the lifeblood of your business, and it is important to build positive relationships with them. The more you know about them and the more they know about and trust you, the more both of you will prosper.

You might be thinking, "This category does not apply to me. I don't have customers or clients."

In my workshops, I often ask, "By a show of hands, how many of you are in sales? How many in customer service? How many are in public relations? How many own and run a business? How many of you manage a team of employees?" Some hands go up.

Then I ask, "How many of you have to convince another person to use an idea of yours? How many of you are looking for a new job, a promotion, a raise?" By the end of my questions, almost everyone has raised his or her hand. The fact is, we are all in sales, customer service, or public relations, regardless of our formal job description.

When you think about it, you are constantly communicating messages and selling your ideas to others. We are all public relations specialists when we act as representatives of our companies or of ourselves. Your "clients" include co-workers, staff, other department heads, and—certainly—your boss. In fact, anyone you "sell" your thoughts or ideas to is a client.

If you are in sales, and we all are, then it is essential to keep customers as happy and profitable members of your network. Besides being the lifeblood of your current business, they can also be your

CREATING CUSTOMER CHEERFULNESS

Here are some networking tactics to keep your customers satisfied:

- Know them. Find out their hobbies, names of family members, likes and dislikes, birthdays, anniversaries, even their favorite foods. Keep good records of this information and use it to build on your relationships.

- Keep in touch. Share information and ideas with customers when you think it will help them. Even if nothing develops, it will provide an opportunity to be on their radar screen. Remember, your goal is to make lasting impressions.

- Handle complaints and concerns promptly. Take responsibility for problems no matter who caused them. Your customers will see you as their lifesaver and will want to help you in return.

- Prove that you are dependable. When you make promises, keep them! This builds trust, an important factor in any relationship.

advocate by referring you to prospects, thereby helping your business to grow and prosper. And you can do the same for them.

As I walked into my doctor's office, he came out front. I am always impressed how he greets each patient by name, no matter how full the waiting room is. As I was called in and walked back to the exam room, I passed by his office, and there on his desk was my book, *Nonstop Networking*.

I said to him a few minutes later, "Dr. S., you are good!" He looked at me curiously, and I explained. "Well, here I was coming today, and you pulled out my book to put right on your desk. That's great and makes me feel important." He smiled and said, "Andrea, I've got to tell you, it's been there since you gave it to me six months ago! It's a great paperweight, and other people always pick it up and ask about it!"

Whether you've written a book or not, you can always give others something that will help keep your name in their mind.

Suppliers

Whether you own a business or work in a company, you buy goods and services from suppliers. Think of all the products and services you buy in your business and in your personal life.

Your suppliers can be anyone. Other than your business contacts, they could include your dry cleaner, hairdresser, and even your doctor. Not long ago, when I showed my doctor my first book, *Nonstop Networking*, he suggested that I contact the organization of which his wife was president. I have now done several projects for her organization and others in the same industry.

Another time, my wonderful computer guru overheard me on the phone with someone as he was installing some software and said, "Andrea, I know the head of purchasing of the company you're calling." Turns out they were friends growing up. As you can imagine, having the "referral" from John was a huge help and got me through right away. I also returned a favor to him by introducing him to one of my strategic partner clients, and now he is doing that person's computer work. Remember, this is a two-way street.

Co-Workers and Colleagues

Look around your office and throughout your organization. Some people you know fairly well, they may even be your friends. For the others, you could set a goal to get to know them better. Start your action plan by asking them out for lunch or coffee or volunteer on a task force so that you'll have more interaction with them. The fact is that the people who work with us and know us are another very powerful source for networking.

Janice works in the legal department of a large company and, through her relationships, found a new apartment and a new carpenter and was able to help one of her friends at another company get a job at her organization. How? It all happened through the power of internal networking. She has also gotten into the habit of learning more about her colleagues and co-workers. She says: "One day at lunch with a colleague, I found out that her best friend's husband was the sales director of a company where my sister was interviewing. My sister was very qualified, yet many other people were, too, and the interviewing process was tough. Yet, with the introduction of my colleague's best friend's husband, my sister is now working in the 'job of her dreams.'" More evidence that the concept, "you just never know," applies here. We'll cover more about developing your internal business relationships across departments later.

Yet, too often I hear: "In my company, we work in 'silos.' How can I strengthen my relationships with other departments?" This is a critical question because we all are working for the same bottom line, and each person with whom we interact is someone we can learn from and possibly cooperate with at work. Larger companies often find out too late that one department is working with a prospective client and other departments could add their expertise to help close the sale or move the business along. Sadly, there is no "crossover" discussion, and business is being lost because of it.

You and your co-workers form a "chain of value" that can reach more potential clients than if you work in isolation from each other. You are all internal invaluable resources for one other. You might ask yourself:

- What links do I have with other co-workers and departments?
- Do people know what I could do to help them? And do I know what they do?
- What are our common goals?
- Are we committed to learning from each other's ideas and creating new possibilities together?

One law firm that I work with realized that it could have developed more business if more of the partners and associates learned more about each other's practice areas. I put a workshop together for the firm, and in the pre-work, I asked the members what questions they had about their firm's other departments. Each attorney came to the program with a mission statement of what his or her department did and suggestions on how all of them could work more productively with other areas.

At the end of the program, each person walked out with someone from another practice area with whom he or she was charged with staying in touch to see what new opportunities could develop. The challenge after these events is always whether people will get out of their comfort zone and change. Most lawyers—as all professionals—are already overworked, yet this internal networking was important and was bottom line-oriented. Partners saw how they could gain new business. I'm happy to report that I stayed in touch with this law firm and, after six months, two new pieces of business were developed—all from the internal relationships we'd established.

A Networking Challenge for You

We can all do this. Right now think about your own internal teams and see where you could uncover new business opportunities right in your own backyard while, at the same time, make everyone better team players.

People in Your Business or Profession

I enjoy developing relationships with other people in my line of work. Some people view them as competitors, and in some ways we are, yet we can also refer, help, and leverage our relationships with each other. I know, for example, that often when I am called for a large project I must bring in a team of trainers. Because I continually develop strong relationships with other consultants, I always have a "team" of people waiting. They feel the same way, and at times I work with them as part of their virtual "group." By removing our egos we both make room for more new business.

I have developed contacts in companies that were not initially interested in my services. Yet, because I was working with others in my business who already had relationships with those businesses, they now see what I can do to help them. Mary is a perfect example. She also runs a training business and has hired me on several occasions to team up with her to do a part of the program where I have expertise. Another time, I called on an executive coach friend of mine to do a project for one of my clients. It all boils down to the fact that I trust these people, and I know their work. We have formed great strategic alliances.

STARTING A NEW JOB

One young man with whom I have worked really goes out of his way to learn about people and their interests. When Pete took a new job, one of the first things he did was to draw a map of his new office area with each cubicle and office noted. As he met people, he wrote down their names on the corresponding space on his map, along with interesting things he learned about them in conversation: the names of their children, their favorite vacation spots, their sports and other outside interests, and favorite restaurants as well as work information. Pete created a foundation for strong business relationships with these people right from the start.

You can do the same. Start to observe the people you know in your business and profession. They can become your network of advisors, and their connections will be very helpful after you build a relationship with them.

Obvious places to meet people in your profession are in business meetings, at conferences, association meetings, trade shows, and wherever people gather formally or informally to share ideas and news about your industry. As you become more successful in your profession, join trade associations and special interest groups; attend seminars, workshops, and conventions; and become an active participant in these programs and groups.

Be willing to share your experience and expertise with those you are getting to know. Think of it this way: a fist clenching tightly onto what it has is unable to grab new opportunities. Be open to others and you can receive from them. Such was the case with Joyce, a very successful trainer and someone I have shared with generously. Because of our business relationship, she referred me to one of her clients to speak at a conference. Joyce knows me and my work, and she knew that I would honor her client relationship and be sure to keep her in the loop and make her a heroine for finding me to speak at the conference. We also have a business relationship and alliance. Want this technique to work for you? Find one professional contact whose business you'll offer to help grow.

People You Went to School with or Met at a Workshop or Seminar

I am involved with my college alumni organization and was asked to speak at one of its meetings. The contacts I reopened there led me to opportunities in two new industries, and I was asked to return to my former college campus to speak with the students. This came about because a former classmate of mine, now one of the managing directors of a large securities company, heard me speak at a conference and referred me to my college's business school. Take a closer look at your alumni magazine with an eye toward people who can help you or whom you can help in your profession. Make sure also to keep the college magazine abreast of achievements along the way for inclusion in the publication. You never know with whom you may reconnect.

My publisher's niece, a recent graduate of a leading technical college, launched a successful career as a photographer's stylist in New York City based almost solely on contacts with alumni of her school. She actually knew very few of them before moving to the city, yet she sought them out and found them willing to help her because they were fellow alumni. At a recent workshop, a young woman named Sarah mentioned, "Everything that has happened to me since college is a result of the people I met in classes and my sorority."

In another instance, a good friend had just landed a large project with the U.S. Air Force. I asked her how she got connected, and she said, "Andrea, this goes back to a friend in my college sorority. Of course, it didn't happen overnight. We've been friends and always found ways to stay connected." Just for the record, my friend has been out of school for at least twenty years. It pays to stay in touch.

At my exercise class, I always talk with Norma, who is in the public relations business. As a result of our talking and "dealing with the stress of the heavy weights," we have gotten to know each other. Over time, she invited me to speak at an association lunch. It was great, and I then connected with two people at that meeting who have since hired me for several media training assignments—all because Norma and I shared weights in exercise class. Of course, I always keep her in the loop whenever an opportunity comes up as a result of her help.

YOU ALREADY HAVE A MUCH LARGER NETWORK THAN YOU THINK

Curious about how big your current network might be? Find out by answering these questions.

- How many people do you work with now?
- How many people have you worked with in the past?
- How many clients do you have?
- How many people do you know from professional organizations?
- How many people do you know from other organizations such as health clubs, your homeowners association, or your children's school groups?
- How many people do you know from your religious affiliations or organizations?
- How many professionals (e.g., doctors, lawyers, accountants) do you come in contact with?
- How many former schoolmates do you stay in touch with?
- How many people do you know in your neighborhood?
- How many friends and relatives do you have?

Add them up. Chances are you have a large network of contacts already.

Meeting Ross is an example of giving a little and getting much in return. He sat in the front row of a seminar where I had donated my time to give a speech at the meeting of a nonprofit professional association. After the program, he sent me a note and we stayed in touch. Talk about a wonderful note writer, Ross wins the award. I'm always getting cards and articles of interest from him. He takes the time to really stay in touch. After about a year, I was invited in to work with his team at one of his company's sales meetings. I got to help Ross out, too. I took a real estate course myself, ran into someone he used to work with, and reconnected them!

Like-Minded People

I find the easiest people to talk to are those who have common interests and ambitions, or who share similar life experiences. And not just professionally; after all, you have a personal life! There are language classes, charity groups where you really believe in the cause, kids' soccer games and recitals, vacations, and religious groups. The people you find at these events and places like the same things you do, and that leads to a perfect networking opportunity.

I love jewelry. It is a fact, and anyone who knows me will agree. It's something I inherited from my mother, who puts me to shame with her collection. You may wonder what this has to do with my business. One day, one of my former clients asked me to have breakfast with him and his friend, Dan, who had been the publisher of a jewelry magazine and was now looking for another position. We had a very interesting meeting and, because I was engrossed in the subject matter of the jewelry industry, I was able to give him some leads. We've stayed in touch. He, in turn, "saved my life" because he happened to call my office several months later, and I answered the phone instead of leaving at that moment for a meeting. I am so glad I did. It was the day of the New York Blackout of 2003, and had I left a minute earlier, I might still be stuck in the elevator of my building (not a good thought!).

Anyway, over the next several months, Dan landed a great job with the top magazine in the jewelry industry. It just so happened that its editorial offices were in Bangkok and I was going to be visiting there. Dan put me in touch with the chief editor, David, and I am now happy to report that I am a contributor and columnist to the magazine on how to develop new business. It's great, because as I write for them on the very topics we are discussing here—how to find, grow, and keep your business—I'm doing it for an industry that I am personally interested in and I have fun doing it. Also, imagine all the new people who will learn about me from reading my articles. In fact, I've already been booked for and delivered two great projects in this industry because new clients saw my articles.

What do you really enjoy, and how can you start to create some new connections for business in that area? Find ways to be visible. Write an article or make a presentation on your area of expertise at a business function where potential clients will be.

Neighbors

Neighbors can serendipitously become valuable members of your network. My publisher, for instance, has found many of her best authors in the small town where she lives. Many of us, however, could get to know our neighbors better. Too often we just wave as they drive by or we chat about our gardens, traffic, or the weather. Living in New York City, sometimes I only see people in the mailroom or elevator, where most people seem to avoid eye contact.

Start an experiment to take relationships with your neighbors to a new level. Go beyond the back fence or mailroom conversations and really get to know them by using some of the techniques you would use at a business networking event. You might be surprised to find a neighbor who is in the same business, or a related one, or who knows someone you want to meet. Of course, good neighbors are always an invaluable source for such things as cleaning services, yard people, painters, electricians, plumbers, or decorators, and when the time comes to move away, realtors. If you're reading this and thinking, "I need some down time," I understand—take the best and leave the rest!

NETWORKING IN YOUR ELEVATOR

One morning in the elevator of my apartment building I noticed a neighbor wearing a T-shirt with the logo of a company I knew very well. I asked her if she worked there, started a conversation, and before we reached the lobby, we found that we both knew several people at her company. In fact, I had worked with another division of her firm, and she was great friends with my main client there. I got to know her, and later, she introduced me to several other contacts at her organization. In addition, she was the president of an industry group I was just joining, and in which I have become more involved.

When my Chicago friend meets someone new in his office building, he looks at what floor the person has pushed and says, "Hi, my name is Tom. May I ask what you do on the seventh floor?" He makes great new connections in less than thirty seconds.

Friends

Friends make the world a happier place. We need to welcome and nurture these people in our lives as well as consider them as important members of our network. What better advocate can we have, or can we be, than a friend? Take time to nurture and cultivate your friends. And network with them in a positive way, never with expectations. Give without the thought of receiving or keeping score, and you will receive the greatest gift of all, a good friend. When something more comes of it, consider that a gift, too.

My friend, Bill, a financial adviser, is one of those people who always looks to find ways to help his friends. He is totally giving of himself and never looks for a payback. Yet he receives them all the time. Why? Because he stays on everyone's radar screen, and when anyone wants a financial adviser, he immediately comes to mind. I know that I look for ways to introduce him to others and for opportunities that would be good for his business. I also trust him and admire his knowledge of his field and the pride he takes in his work. I know that he would do a great job in any project he undertakes.

How do you find the time to see your friends? Make plans to meet for breakfast, lunch, or dinner. Even better, look for unusual activities to share. I have met friends for manicures, for afternoon tea, for shopping excursions, for workouts at the gym (you can definitely chat on the treadmill or bike—it's also good for your heart!), for walks or runs. Go to a sports event, play golf (the ultimate traditional networking activity), or have a drink together after work.

Family

Network with your family? Why not? A friend of mine recently told me she recommended her nephew, a graphic artist, for a project for her company. She was familiar with his work and was confident he could do a quality job, quote a reasonable price, and meet the deadlines. Remember, her reputation was at stake, as it would have been with any recommendation she made. She also wisely distanced herself from the financial negotiations. Both she and her nephew were very clear with one another that this was a business arrangement and, no matter the outcome, it would remain so. In this case, it worked out just fine. He did a good job, as she knew he would, and has received several subsequent assignments.

My cousin, Helen, opened the door for me at a law firm where she had worked. She made the introduction and then said, "Go for it." She made it clear that she could only open the door; it was up to me to make it happen.

On the other hand, I have also opened the door for her with several other projects and contacts. Now Helen is an organizational consultant and has helped me a lot, so I'm always very happy to refer clients to her. Networking with your family can work. Just make sure to maintain your integrity and be mindful of the reputations involved.

One more note, if you read my first book, *Nonstop Networking*, you heard me talk about my wonderful dentist, Dr. Miller who has been my dentist for almost as long as I've had teeth. He is also my cousin, and I am always happy to refer patients to him. As my grandmother used to say, "He has a very light touch" as he works on your teeth. Just recently, at a cocktail party, a couple mentioned they lived in the same community as Dr. Miller, and I asked if they had heard of him. It was great. The wife goes to him, and the husband was impressed because Dr. Miller referred him to an excellent specialist for work my cousin doesn't do. Again—networking at its finest.

People You Meet by Chance

This is where the fun starts. These people seem to come into your life by chance and from almost any place: on planes and trains, at the grocery store, at Starbucks. To make these chance encounters work for you, treat those you meet as important people to have in your network. I believe there are no accidents. People come into our lives for reasons, sometimes just to teach us something. Keep your ears and eyes open for these opportunities.

While visiting a friend in the hospital in Florida, I was sitting in the waiting room and started talking with the woman next to me. I was fascinated by her time management and organizational skills, even in the hospital waiting room.

As we talked she described her business and the type of clients she worked with. By the time I was allowed into my friend's room, I had made a new contact and had already referred her to two new business projects. And from her, I learned about the perfect organizational device to help me work better.

One time in a New York taxi on my way to a dinner party, I started chatting with the driver, who told me that he loved the people of New York because they were so helpful. I learned during our ten-block long ride (you might know about New York City traffic) that he was a lawyer from another country. When he arrived in the United States, he had to start over in law school, and at the same time he was working as a paralegal and driving a cab to support his family. Talk about determination. I gave him my card and asked him to e-mail me his resume to see if there was anything I could do. I first wanted to see if he would follow up and whether he was for real. Well, he did and he does have the credentials. I have already sent his information to two people. You never know what will happen, yet I'm sure my driver, Sangiv, will find some wonderful opportunities. I'm so glad that I was in his cab and, as always, had on my networking eyes and ears. You just never know!

Reconnect with People You Already Know

Make a game plan for reconnecting with those already in your network. Start with a list of people, in each of the ten categories we just discussed, who will take your phone call. Now give them a call. For what reason, you may ask. You call just to touch base, to say hello, to catch up on what has been happening in each other's lives.

This happened to me recently. I received two wonderful calls from people who were from "history." They had both read an article of which I had been the subject, and they went to my Web site and then called me. One was from my first sales job, and he was the president of the company at the time. Although I knew him somewhat, all these many years later, it was so nice to hear from him, and, as it turns out, I may do some work for his company. The other was from a woman who had worked for me when I was publisher of a magazine. She called to say how excited she was to reconnect. We caught up, and I found out that she has her own business. I've already sent some people to her store, which, by the way, sells jewelry!

When you make that first call, instead of feeling awkward, keep in mind the positive impact. The person may have been thinking of you and meaning to call. This has happened to me countless times. These calls are easy to make because you're not going to be asking for anything. Be prepared. If you've been out of touch for a while, the person may respond with, "What do you want?" or you know he or she is thinking that. Imagine the person's surprise and pleasure when this turns out to be purely a friendly call.

Identify Key Business Contacts You Would Like to Meet

Make a list of key people in your industry or profession you'd like to meet. These should be specific individuals—or specific titles of individuals if you don't know the name of the current person in that position—within an organization or industry group that would be beneficial to your career or business goals. Aim high! Include high-level executives and high-profile people in your field.

Do your research and determine at which organization, interest group, or place you could meet them. Think about people they know, people you know, and the possible connections that might lead to a meeting. No connection is impossible.

One new woman in my network, Karen, owns a graphic arts company. She and I met on the chance that we might have opportunities to work with one another or with people each of us knew.

I liked Karen's style and sent four letters of introduction to some of my clients for her. She, in turn, wrote a great letter of introduction to

Here's a game plan you can practice. I call it my FOUR-mula for Success.

Call four people per week from your list, including a:

1. Client or prospect with whom you have not been in touch for awhile
2. Former business colleague
3. Friend you haven't heard from recently
4. Current friend

The last call, to a current friend, will be the easiest, most fun, and a reward for making the other three. As you work through your list, you will find that all past relationships become current ones. Then, keep it going. It's easy to fit four calls a week into your busy schedule. It breaks down the formidable task of reconnecting with your contacts into manageable, bite-size tasks—baby steps, as I like to call it. Make it a practice you continue to use as your network grows. Most important will be the results. Imagine, once you've solidified your relationship, how simple it will be to ask later if you ever need a favor.

one of her clients that I have always wanted to work with. When I made my initial call, I got right through, and the process of working with the client is steadily underway. I knew this company and the person I wanted to talk with, yet I didn't have a connection until Karen referred me.

You see how we have all sorts of people in our network without even realizing it. We have also looked at who you need to get to know to strengthen your contact base. In the next chapter, you'll be getting ready to "step out" to the places where you'll have a great time networking with current and new contacts. Before you rush out the door, however, take some time to look into your current network with the following exercise. It will lay a foundation for many opportunities in the future.

Exercise: Who Is in Your Current Network?

This exercise is designed to help you bring to mind the people in your current network. When you think long enough about the people you have connected with throughout your life, you'll realize that you're in a much better position than you might have thought.

Your Immediate Network

This network includes people who would answer or return a call from you quickly. For each type of person, name up to three people you would consider as part of your immediate network.

Customers of clients

1. _____

2. _____

3. _____

People from whom you buy products or services

1. _____

2. _____

3. _____

Co-workers

1. _____

2. _____

3. _____

Professional colleagues

1. _____

2. _____

3. _____

Friends and neighbors

1. _____

2. _____

3. _____

People in Your Secondary Network

Your secondary network includes people you connect with periodically. They might include people you went to school with, worked with at a previous job, friends from an old neighborhood, or people you have met by chance and found interests in common. List up to ten people in this category, and beside each name, note how you met the person.

1. _____

2. _____

3. _____

4. _____

5. _____

6. _____

7. _____

8. _____

9. _____

10. _____

People in Your Universal Network

If you had to make a list of everyone you know, how many people would be on it? Chances are it would be a much longer list than the names above in your immediate and secondary networks. This long list of your universal network is something to go back to every few months to see what has changed in your business life that would warrant getting in touch

Say you have several medical industry contacts you have not worked with for years. Right now they could be part of your universal network. If you change jobs, however, and start working with medical products, these people would be moved to your secondary or immediate network. Your network is a living list that needs to be nurtured and maintained.

Networking Ladder:

Top Rung: Your immediate network: people who will take a call from you right away

Middle Rung: Your secondary network: people who will know who you are when you contact them

Lower Rung: entire list of everyone you have ever known

Key exercise point: Check this list every three months to make sure you keep your network current. That way, you'll always have a list of people to reach out to when you are looking for a new opportunity or have something to help someone in your network.

"Ideas are a dime a dozen.
People who put them into action are priceless."
—Anonymous

"Patience and perseverance have a magical effect
before which difficulties disappear and obstacles vanish."
—John Quincy Adams

CHAPTER 2

Where to Meet People

> "The secret of getting ahead is getting started.
>
> The secret of getting started is breaking your complex overwhelming tasks into small manageable tasks and then starting on the first one." —**Mark Twain**

Where do people you want to know gather? Identify the kinds of places, events, associations, trade organizations, and conferences where people in your profession, or the professions you are interested in, meet. These are the types of places where people get together to exchange information, contacts, and knowledge or just to enjoy each other's company.

Make a list. What do you already know about these organizations? Do you belong to them and attend meetings? If so, how can you get more out of the organization? Would you like to know more about these organizations and their members to find others that will help you build your network?

If you need to start a list from scratch, think first about your own interests and passions. Do you go to your kids' parent-teacher meetings, watch their soccer games, lead their scout troop? Do you belong to your neighborhood association or local historic group, sing in the choir at your church or synagogue, work out at a local health club? Do you like to travel?

Do you volunteer or contribute to charities? Do you belong to a book club? Do you take dance, art, language classes? Thinking that trade shows and business meetings are the only places to go is too limiting. Some people start up lifelong friendships or even business partnerships from a chance meeting far away from a business environment.

Events and Organizations

There are several types of events where you can meet business contacts. The first that comes to mind is the structured event where the stated purpose is to network. These events can take place at associations and industry-specific group events as well as at meetings of networking organizations. People who attend these events expect to introduce themselves and talk about what they do in hopes of making a helpful business connection. In some ways, it's easier to network at these events since that is their stated purpose. However, if you think you are going to make contacts of a lifetime after a few of these meetings, you'll be disappointed. Building solid relationships takes time. These types of events are a perfect place to start learning a little about the people you'd liked to connect with down the road. These exchanges can start the process of building trust, and people do business with those they trust.

Another opportunity to meet and make connections is at association and industry events. Here, the stated purpose is either to conduct business or to address a specific topic of interest to the group. Although many people attend to "network," the event is not structured around that activity. There may be more opportunities to make solid connections here.

These industry organizations also hold social and cultural events either specifically meant for networking or for other stated purposes, such as to raise money for a charity or to recognize industry leaders. So, when you start getting involved in any group, there are often several opportunities to pursue.

The key is to find the right group (or groups) for you. Then, get involved, attend meetings, and build relationships. Below are descriptions of the various types of groups you may want to consider.

Associations and Industry-Specific Organizations

I grew up in the direct marketing industry. Like any industry, it has many different forums, councils, and meetings, just for that industry. Plenty of contacts, relationships, and business opportunities are developed at these events. Networking, however, is the byproduct of these functions, and it always happens when you keep your ears and eyes open!

Generally, the stated mission of the organization is educational, informational, or, for some trade associations, reviewing industry trends to see what future opportunities there might be. Most are open to those who work in, or who aspire to work in, the industry or profession they represent. All provide a wide variety of services to members, including the opportunity to meet and connect with like-minded people. And just by being involved, you will meet people with whom you will feel rapport and might build a relationship.

You can find these groups and trade associations easily by asking others in your business or profession or by reading trade magazines. Do an Internet search for organizations you know about and type key words in a search engine to find others. When you find one you think you'll like, be sure to check out its "links" or "resources" page. Often they may have links to other organizations in the industry that may interest you. Many have local chapters, which you will find on their home Web page. Or look in the *American Society of Association Executives Directory*, which lists more than twenty-three thousand organizations with contact information, including Web sites. You can access this directory from the American Society of Association Executives' Web site at www.asaenet.org. Look under directories/associations, then enter your industry to get a list of organizations. Or you can find this directory at your local public library.

TWO THAT WORKED FOR ME

Since I began my consulting company, I have been a member of two fine organizations: Financial Women's Association and Advertising Women of New York. Through the years, I have found clients, suppliers, friends, and mentors through these groups. I did not join them specifically because they are women's organizations; I joined them because they represented two industries I work in and wanted to learn more about. After I did my research and attended some meetings, both of these organizations kept coming to the top of my list.

Although I have reaped many rewards from these associations, I believe it is all about giving first. Getting involved on committees, doing workshops and showcases, and helping others along the way opened many doors for me. I always know that what gets remembered, gets rewarded. The "it's a small world" effect holds true here. I have met countless people at these associations who connected me to businesspeople I never would have met on my own. My secret? I take the time to get involved, instead of just being a spectator.

Joining and becoming active in one or several of these groups will provide you with many profitable networking opportunities and will give your career a boost.

Networking Organizations

These are groups where the primary stated purpose is to network and to exchange leads, contacts, and tips. Most are not industry-specific. In fact, they usually like to have members in different fields to grow more business opportunities. Some examples are:

- Business Network International (BNI), www.bni.com
- Leads Club, HYPERLINK www.leadsclub.com
- Le Tip International, Inc., www.letip.com
- National Association of Female Executives (NAFE), www.nafe.com
- ExecuNet, www.ExecuNet.com
- The Five O'Clock Club, www.FiveO'ClockClub.com
- The Financial Executives Networking Group, www.thefeng.org
- Forty Plus, www.FortyPlus.org

Some of these groups are national in scope, and many have local chapters with anywhere from five to five hundred members. Remember, you seldom have to become a member to attend a meeting. Most allow guests or visitors to come to determine if the organization is a good fit for them.

Meeting schedules vary greatly. They can take place at early-morning breakfasts or right after work. Many allow some or all attendees to give a thirty-second talk about their businesses (the elevator pitch) and the type of clients they hope to find. Some meetings might even allow for member showcases where time is allowed for a person to discuss his or her business in more detail to make it easier for others to refer clients. The hope is that you will be thinking of your friends at all times and make connections for them that they may never have had otherwise.

Some networking organizations hold their members accountable. They might even keep track of who is giving contacts to and getting contacts from each other. If someone is only getting leads and not giving, the organization may question whether to keep that person on as a member.

What results can you expect? It depends on how much you and other members of your group are willing to contribute. If I had to offer a formula, I would say that:

networking organization you like
+ frequent attendance
+ giving more than you get
+ following up with new contacts
+ reporting back to the person who gave you the contact
= networking success.

The best thing about these groups is that they are structured and usually have a facilitator who gets everyone to follow an agenda. This format seems to work well for many people, especially those of us who are introverted or just uncomfortable with the notion of networking or asking for referrals. You can be great at your particular work or trade, yet not be comfortable with this way of building your business. Let me show you how one of these groups works.

Two years ago, I was asked to be a lunch speaker for The Executive's Association of Greater New York—EAGNY. I walked into a room of eighty-five people, all owners or principals of mid-size businesses, who come together weekly to share information and leads and help with each other's business. They were adept at networking, and here I was speaking to this group! I was daunted at first because I realized that they all thought of themselves as expert networkers. I quickly adapted my speech to show how they could help coach their staffs to network and find new clients. As a result, they invited me to become their official "networking guru." This group is terrific. Some of the members have been together more than twenty years, and the organization is international. I have made great connections and have gotten some terrific and trustworthy "suppliers" from the group, including a terrific gourmet caterer, my new Blackberry PDA, and a wonderful cruise line.

I now have the opportunity to go out and represent this group as one of its spokespeople. The system truly works—it's built on hardworking professionals, all experts in their fields, who come together to learn from and do business with their colleagues. Also, many wonderful friendships have been formed over the years.

Other networking groups, such as The Five O'Clock Club, Forty Plus, and ExecuNet, focus on job hunting. They are invaluable resources for networking and offer helpful tips and leads. These groups host meetings for networking, publish newsletters, and provide workshops and seminars to aid in job searches. In some cases, the group's Web site alone is an invaluable resource. A quick search on the Internet will yield similar sites, many of which will be specific to your industry and interests.

Internal (Company) Meetings and Events

An important, yet often overlooked, opportunity for meeting and developing contacts is the internal business meeting or social event within your company. Recognizing the value of employees' internal networking, one company I know of invited me to present at its annual meeting, and we started off with an exercise that has since become tradition for the group.

The company's employees start the first evening of their sales conference with this assignment. Each person is to find someone at the opening cocktail party event whom he or she doesn't know well and learn something new about the person. This builds a foundation for forming new alliances and contacts. The company has found that this simple exercise helps its associates work well together throughout the conference as well as later when they return to their home offices. It also improves interactions with senior staff members.

Every company has internal meetings. Much as we may dread them, meetings are necessary for conducting business and opening lines of communication. Many companies recognize the importance of using these meetings for internal networking as well. Several months ago I was invited into a corporation to conduct a workshop on "The How-Tos of Internal Networking" for 375 employees from different departments at all job levels. I approached the assignment with the thought that they were all like-minded people with a shared interest in the company's goals and mission. I was able to discuss the opportunities and advantages of meeting and developing associations with people across the firm, regardless of their position or title. For meeting and getting to know each other, I used exercises incorporating the tips and techniques for a successful event (found in chapter 3).

I have also done this for law and accounting firms where many people tend to work in what are sometimes referred to as "silos," as we discussed in chapter 1, and who rarely think of the resources available to them in other parts of their organization. I get many e-mails and notes from people after these workshops telling me how they connected and got to know someone in another department and how much this has helped them in their work and enabled them to help others as well.

One exercise that works well for a company meeting is to have every person drop his or her business card into a bowl. When people leave the meeting, they take out a card, and their assignment is to call that person, introduce themselves, ask what their goal was from the meeting or session, and then set a follow-up date to call in two weeks. When the system works correctly, two calls are made; you make one, and someone else calls you. This is a great way to have some internal team building, learn from each other, and make each meeting count. Try this in your own organization or department.

Everywhere Else

Finally, there is everywhere else. Classes, seminars, and workshops that are industry-related and where you go to further your skills are prime networking opportunities. Doing volunteer work or joining a neighborhood association or the board of your church or synagogue also provides opportunities to meet people you need in your network. Here's a caveat, however: avoid joining just to network, thinking you'll get quick results. It won't happen. Follow your interest first. Then enjoy yourself, learn a new skill, make a contribution, and meet new contacts while you're at it. Here are some ideas for you, depending on your interests.

Service Groups

The mission of most nonprofit service organizations is to help others who are less fortunate. Though they are not traditional networking groups, their members come from various walks of life, rather than from one business, and many could become members of your network. Some such organizations include:

- Rotary Clubs
- Lions Clubs
- Kiwanis
- Chambers of Commerce
- Political clubs such as Democratic or Republican clubs
- League of Women Voters
- Charitable or fund-raising groups
- Museums and art leagues
- Religious groups
- Parent-teacher associations
- Homeowners associations

One service organization is Lighthouse for the Blind. My friend, Leslie, got involved with this group in a most unusual way. She loves guinea pigs and had one as a pet for years, yet, when she got married, it was either her husband or the pig! Of course, she picked her husband. However, she started to visit a pet store all the time after work and befriended a new little guinea pig there. When the little guy was sold, the shop owners, who knew Leslie well by this time, told the new owners about her.

MAKING AN INTEREST PAY OFF

A great example of making an interest pay off has been a realtor I worked with on an article for the Women's Council of Realtors (WCR). Kathy is an active member of WCR. She is also actively involved on the March of Dimes board in her community and in her church. Being part of these local groups has helped her build credibility in her community and it has also helped her real estate business. When people see that you are part of the community, and a contributor to its welfare, they will begin to trust you. You will become known to them as "the" expert in your area of work, and they will eventually start coming to you for your advice when the need arises. This can lead to business opportunities with them or their recommending you to their friends and colleagues. Remember, you join these groups because you are sincerely interested and believe in them. However, you're always willing to give friendly advice or offer your services to those you know you can help.

Ironically, they also lived in the same neighborhood, and Leslie would go over to visit "Sandy" the guinea pig. Fast forward two years. She has become great friends with the new owner, Sarah, who is also a senior volunteer at the Lighthouse. Leslie now sits on the board and is very involved and active. Again—an unusual, yet true and wonderful, story.

The following are some of the largest organizations that provide service to those in need:

- Lutheran Services in America
- YMCA
- Salvation Army
- United Jewish Communities
- American Red Cross
- Catholic Charities USA
- Goodwill Industries International
- Boys and Girls Clubs

Whether you belong to any of these and leverage them as a networking resource depends on your interests and your inclination to volunteer your time and expertise to your community. These groups exist to serve the community; meeting and connecting with people is a bonus. As I have said, like-minded people are the people you want in your network. You will find these people at these organizations. In addition, at many charitable and fund-raising events, you will find executives and other business leaders who volunteer their time. What better way to get to know them and for them to get to know your abilities than to work on such an event? Join, volunteer, and profit from these organizations.

Special Interest Groups and Activities

There are networking opportunities everywhere, even at your gym, book club, chess club, salsa dance class, round-robin racquetball game, Wednesday evening church fellowship group, and the exotic vacation destination of your choice. Though all of these groups are personally rewarding, they can help you make connections with like-minded people who could become valuable members of your network. I recall a friend worrying about an organized tour of Europe she was about to embark on: "What if I don't like any of the people I meet?"

"You will like them," I replied. "They enjoy the same things you do or they would have chosen another tour."

I was right. She had a great time and came back with new friends plus a number of professional contacts that subsequently benefited her business.

It's Not Just about the Event— Get Involved

To grow your network, you must do more than just join an organization. You have to get involved to meet new people and make a name for yourself. Here is my three-step process for involving yourself in any organization where you've identified people you want to know.

1. Go to meetings, meet people, and then *join* the organization(s) that best suit you.

2. Volunteer, join a committee, *become active*.

3. Write an article, give a speech, *become known*.

Go to Meetings, Meet People, and Join the Organization(s) that Best Suit You

As I've said before, if you're going to invest time and energy in an organization, make sure it's the best one for you. Most organizations encourage a prospective member to attend a couple of meetings before joining. I highly recommend this, no matter what you think you may already know about the organization. Use your networking techniques and set a goal to meet at least two new people at each meeting you attend. Then set up a follow-up meeting with each person you met to get to know him or her and to find out more about the organization.

You'll discover from their answers whether future meetings will help you achieve your reasons for joining the organization. Yes, it's true that you always need to be open to connecting with people. However, you also have to make the most of your resources—your time and money.

Ask to see a list of past and future programs. Are these of interest and benefit to you? Are the speakers people you want to hear and meet? Are other programs and workshops offered that would be of interest and that would help you in your profession? Is there a newsletter? Check out the group's Web site. Is it useful and informative? Would you have something to contribute to a newsletter or a program?

For each group or activity you consider, ask yourself:
- Who attends meetings and actively participates? Are these the people I want in my network?
- Is the group network-friendly, willing to give and share information with others?

- Are the meetings, speakers, and activities of interest and benefit to me?
- What can I contribute that will be of interest and helpful to the group and its members?

Once you feel satisfied with the answers to these questions, sign up! Join and become an active member.

MY 2-2-2 STRATEGY

Before you decide to join a group:

- Attend two meetings.
- Meet two people and exchange business cards.
- Arrange two follow-up meetings for breakfast, lunch, or coffee.

This does two things: You'll find out if you want to join the organization, and you'll expand your network by two.

Volunteer, Join a Committee, Become Active

Meeting people is the reason you join an organization. Becoming actively involved in what the organization does will speed up the process.

Join the program committee, for instance, one of the most interesting and profitable committees in any organization. As an active member of this committee, you'll meet and interact with all of the speakers and presenters—the experts in your field. Who in your industry would you like to meet but have no logical way to do so? Invite the person to do a program for your organization, and you'll be on his or her radar screen.

If the program committee doesn't seem right for you, join another one that interests you. You will meet and get to know more people in a shorter time, and they will get to know you. When you only attend meetings, you limit your ability to meet and get to know members of the organization. After all, the majority of the time spent at a meeting is devoted to the program, which usually involves listening to a great speaker.

Or how about volunteering to be the "greeter"? The greeter meets everyone who attends the meeting, so you are guaranteed a chance to introduce yourself to everyone. Then you will have an opening line to connect with them again later in the meeting. I love to do this, and it is a sure way to meet people.

TEACH A CLASS

A speech or presentation can be as simple as teaching a class in a topic you know. In addition to speaking and teaching in corporations, I keep myself fresh with the courses I teach at New York University on self marketing and at Baruch College on networking to international MBA students. My students come from many different professions and industries. For example, last year my classes included a store owner, an attorney from a major firm, the owner of a mid-size advertising agency, an intern at a large public relations firm, a seasoned orthodontist, an international banker, and a weekly news magazine editor, to name a few. It was wonderful to see these people making connections among themselves. I felt like I was the real winner in all of this. In this class, as in so many others I've taught, I made friends and business connections. My network continues to expand.

Become active in the organizations you join. Doing so will expand your network quickly and efficiently.

Write an Article, Give a Speech, and Become Known

One of the best ways to get your name in front of the members of an organization is to get your name into print. Remember how you checked out the organization's newsletter and Web site before you joined to see whether you could make a contribution? Now you know about the types of articles that are published in the newsletter or on the Web site, and it's time to make that contribution. Write an article and submit it to the editor or webmaster. Even if your article is just a recap of the last meeting, do it, get a byline, and get it published. You will start to gain name recognition and, as I say, "Repetition causes recognition." It will be easier to meet people when they remember your article and your professional credentials, which were mentioned in that article. In addition, you will be making a valued contribution to the organization and its members.

Giving a speech or presentation to your organization is another way to become known and meet more people. Organizations are always looking for program ideas or breakout sessions for larger meetings or conventions. Show them your expertise and seize the opportunity to become a presenter on some topic you think could be of benefit to the group. If you are fearful of public speaking, take a course in presentation skills and practice what you've learned whenever you have an opportunity. The ability to speak in front of a group, as tough as it may be for many of us, is a necessary skill in the business world. I have been teaching presentation skills for more than twenty years to hundreds of clients and thousands of participants, and I can assure you that learning and practicing these skills greatly boosts confidence and ensures success. I practice every single day.

Now that you know where to find the people you want to meet, from neighborhood groups to business newsletters, you're ready to network in the traditional sense—at an event! The next chapter gives you the ins and outs of what to do when it's time to network.

Exercise: Where Can I Meet People?

Make a list of at least three industry-specific organizations that you would like to research for joining and using their Web sites.

1. _____
2. _____
3. _____

List at least three networking-specific organizations you might join.

1. _____
2. _____
3. _____

Make a list of all of your personal interests. How could you combine these with your professional interests?

1. _____
2. _____
3. _____

Make a list of at least three organizations or activities related to your interests in which you would like to participate and to which you can make a contribution.

1. _____
2. _____
3. _____

Make a list of three unusual places where you can talk to new people. (Have fun with this!)

1. _____

2. _____

3. _____

What is your action plan for the next three months?

Where will you go, who will you meet, how will you follow up?

Month one

Month two

Month three

Do your research. Join. Contribute. Meet new contacts!

> *"The world is a great mirror. It reflects back to you what you are. If you are loving, if you are friendly, if you are helpful, the world will prove loving and friendly and helpful to you. The world is what you are."*
>
> **—Thomas Dreier**

CHAPTER 3

Techniques for a Successful Networking Event

Why does the thought of going to a business or industry event sometimes seem so daunting? Often it is because we feel we have to go and network, and we put unnecessary pressure on ourselves. I have even seen grown people break out in a sweat just thinking of what they have to do.

My hope is to help people first discover what makes them feel uncomfortable and then plan the steps they will take to improve their attitude and see how networking can be an excellent experience.

The fact is, few of us learn about networking in a formal sense, or perhaps we did not have a mentor to encourage and show us the way. When we internalize the concept that networking is just a way to learn and help others, does it seem too simple? The issue is that many of us feel we need "permission" to walk up to someone at an event or in another department of our company, introduce ourselves, and begin a conversation. Many people have confided in me that they just don't know how to do it or what to do. Almost everyone asks, "How should I begin?" "What if I look like a fool before senior management?" and "What are they thinking of me?" These are some of the thoughts that bombard them.

How would you feel if your CEO announced at a meeting, "Let's all get to know each other better. I want everyone to network!" What goes through your mind when you attend a networking event at a convention, business meeting, or seminar? What is your attitude when you join an association, trade group, or interest group? Is the answer, "I think I'll just stand off to the side and see what happens," or "I'm going to meet new people today, and it's going to be a great experience." (Fear not if you're not at the point of jumping in to meet new people, because I trust your attitude will change by the time you finish this book.)

To take your own reading on your networking comfort level at events, think about how you would answer these questions:

- Where would I start in a room full of strangers?
- How do I approach another person and introduce myself?
- How would I keep the conversation going?
- How do I even remember the other person's name?
- Will the person think I'm rude if I hand him or her my card and ask for his or hers?
- What if I'm the only new person and everyone else knows each other? Will they think I'm intruding? Will they let me into their group?
- How do I break away from someone so I can keep on mingling?
- If I connect with someone, how do I follow up?

If you've ever asked yourself any of these questions, you're in good company. Many people who attend my seminars and workshops express these feelings about networking events. It's hard to break old habits. When you are unfamiliar with the simple techniques of effective networking, you tend to stay within your comfort zone at these events. It's easier to hang out with friends or to stand in the corner and wait for lunch to begin. Now for a little tough love. Unless you're making new contacts and developing your business, greater success in the future will evade you.

Give Yourself Permission

"You must give yourself *permission* to network," I advise my clients. Many of us lack the self-confidence to walk into a new group. We worry that we'll fail somehow or that people won't like us. We forget that a business event is where people expect to meet and connect with other people. That is why they are there, and adjusting your mind-set to a positive one is the first step to success. Allow yourself to use your confidence to adopt a positive attitude. And you will have more confidence when you're prepared with effective techniques to use when you walk into that room full of people who *do* want to network with you.

Preparation—Before the Event

Give yourself the competitive edge. Prepare yourself before any event by doing the tasks discussed below. You'll feel better and be ready to meet, greet, and connect. In fact, preparation is the key, because it's one way to make sure that you will feel better about yourself and have greater confidence. Just like anything important in life, preparation is 80 percent of success.

Do Your Research

The Internet has made it easy to do pre-event research to find out about the sponsoring company or organization. You can type any topic, person, or organization into a search engine and in seconds have more information than you need. To make all this manageable, look first for the most current material. I check the "press room" or "news center" to find the latest information or the latest press release about the company, person, or industry I am researching.

Read either print or electronic versions of industry, association, and trade magazines and newsletters. I find lots of articles and news items about promotions, job changes, and other news events that present opportunities for me to start a conversation with someone. The extra time you spend on the Internet will be "net worth" it!

At the very least, get a copy of the event flier or program in advance. See who will be speaking and learn as much as you can about the speakers and their topics. If awards are to be presented, do some quick research on the recipients. When you spend some time doing research, you'll be able to develop some opening lines that will make approaching new people much easier.

Have you ever had to make a presentation in college, at work, or for some organization? Networking takes similar preparation. When you are well prepared and know your subject matter, you find yourself much more relaxed when meeting new people who could turn out to be great contacts.

Identify Who You Want to Meet

Before any event, I strategically think of some of the people I want to meet and how to make that happen. Face it, if you go to a two-hour event with, say, three hundred people, it would be physically and mentally impossible even to just say hello to each person. (And if you did do that, you would be what I call a "negative networker.") So, identify a couple of specific people or types of people (e.g., salespeople, human resource directors). Of course, it's great to identify people you already know with whom you can reconnect and use as a springboard to meet others.

The great thing is that you can begin to network the moment you walk in the door by connecting with the person at the registration desk who helped plan the event.

When I'm attending a meeting with a group for the first time, I often call the person who is organizing the event in advance to introduce myself and ask if he or she might be able to introduce me to some other members when I get there. I did this recently, and my "advance" contact, who happened to be the president of the organization, was delighted that I recognized her as I walked in. She was graciously enthusiastic about introducing me to several new contacts. By the way, I knew exactly who she was because I recognized her from her picture on the group's Web site.

At the end of the evening, I thanked her and let her know that I enjoyed meeting the people in her organization. The following day I sent her a note, and she responded with an e-mail inviting me to the next meeting. By doing my research ahead of time and learning something about the people I wanted to meet, I could be more self-assured and relaxed in my conversations with my new contacts.

Have you done that before? If not, look to see what events you are going to in the near future and try out this research technique.

Take Your Tool Kits—Intangible and Tangible

For any event you must have the proper "gear.'" For networking events, I've created a couple of tool kits that are easy to carry with you. They will ensure that all of your interactions and follow-ups will appear seamless and natural. As I say about these or any of my suggestions, remember to take the best that works for you and come up with a few new ideas that will show your "networking personality." And if you're more of a natural networker or one of those people who feels very confident networking, these will only be a reminder for what you already carry with you.

Your Intangible Tool Kit

The first tool kit, which weighs the least yet has the greatest value, includes the intangibles, those "items" that reflect the state of mind you bring with you to these events. Here's what to put in this tool kit:

- **A positive attitude**—Come with a positive outlook; leave your problems and challenges behind. Forget what happened at the office and walk in relaxed and open to opportunity.

- **Self-confidence**—Keep in mind how much you have to offer to those you meet at this event. You're an expert in your field and you want to share your knowledge with your new contacts. I often give myself a mini pep talk before I walk in, something like: "There is someone in this room I can help today," or "Today I will learn something new from someone."

- **An open mind**—Forget your preconceived notions; just go to give and learn without any grand expectations. That will certainly alleviate any pressure. Think of your mind as a sponge: what great new information will you absorb?

- **Your presence**—Before you enter the event, turn off your cell phone, pager (unless you are a doctor on call), and Blackberry. Be present in the here and now and avoid distractions. It shows respect for the people you are speaking with and for the event. When you focus on people, they focus on you.

- **Ears**—Make sure your ears are open and you are ready to listen and learn. Talk less and listen more. We were given two ears and one mouth; remember to use them in that proportion.

- **Eyes**—Be ready to observe. Make eye contact to assure people that they have your full attention and interest.

- **A smile**—This is the universal greeting and the key approachability factor. Plus, we all look more attractive when we're smiling.
- **A firm handshake**—Show that your greeting is sincere with a firm, confident handshake. Make sure it's not a bone crusher or a jellyfish!

Now that you have these "tools" in your kit, remember that networking takes place anywhere and anytime. It's easy to carry your intangible tool kit with you.

Your Tangible Tool Kit

The items in your tangible tool kit will prepare you to meet, connect, and follow up with ease. While these are small items, using them can dramatically improve your image with the people you meet. Your tangible tool kit should contain items like:

- **Breath mints**—It's only polite to be concerned about your breath. I've found that when you are talking a lot, your month becomes dry and the quality of your breath deteriorates over the course of the event. The garlic and onion-smothered meal you ate takes on a whole new aroma after a while.
- **Hand sanitizer**—You will shake a lot of hands during any event and, unfortunately, collect a lot of germs you don't want to pass along. No need to be compulsive, just use it occasionally and subtly. By the way, I did not consult with Donald Trump about this beforehand. He's a great networker and never shakes hands; however, shaking hands isn't likely to go out of style soon.
- **Business cards**—Make sure you have an adequate supply of cards in good condition (without any lint from the bottom of your purse or added creases from your wallet) and within easy reach.

- **Business card case(s)**—Take one for your cards and one for the cards you collect. Keep them in separate pockets. You never want to give away someone else's card accidentally as your own!

- **A nice pen**—Consider this as an accessory and part of your image. I'm always on the lookout for fun, interesting pens since I collect them. They need not be expensive, just make sure they look good. Take two in case the ink runs out and certainly avoid the plastic pens hotels give away.

- **A small notepad**—Use this to jot down what you learn about a new contact. I like to write something about each person to remember and follow up. Don't write on the back of the person's business card, as some cultures consider this rude. Also, use a small pad instead of your large day planner. Make your notes unobtrusively so your new acquaintance doesn't think you're a reporter or spy.

- **Note cards and stamps**—I carry these so I can write my personal follow-up notes immediately after the event. As soon as you get back home or to your hotel room, write a note before you go to bed; otherwise, this valuable opportunity to show your interest will disappear.

- **Highlighter**—I use this to highlight my name on my nametag. People always ask me, "How did you get your name highlighted so that it stands out?" It's a conversation starter.

- **Name tag**—Wear this on your right side so that people will see your name as they shake your right hand.

- **Mirror**—Take a quick look before walking into the event to make sure you have a big smile and nothing between your teeth, that your hair is tidy, and that no tags are sticking out of your collar.

I welcome learning about any other "tools" for better networking. Let me know what else works for you to make the process seamless. Go to www.mybusinessrelationships.com and send me your comments through my contact link.

Have an Opening Line

Think about what you will say in advance of meeting someone new. Prepare several opening lines and practice them in front of the mirror at home. Then, when you use them at an event, they'll easily flow off your tongue. And the more you do it, the more confident you'll become.

Here are some "opening lines" to consider:

- "I'm thinking of joining this group. Are you a member? What do you think of its programs (meetings, get-togethers, resources, etc.)?"
- "What brought you to this meeting?"
- "I'm new here. What can you tell me about this group?"
- "How does this first meeting at this convention (seminar, conference) compare to others you've attended?"
- "Do you find these meetings helpful to your business?"
- "Have you heard the speaker before? What do you know about her?"
- "What are some of the benefits of this association?"
- "That's a great suit, tie, pin (etc.). Where did you get it?"
- "Hello, I don't think we've met yet, I'm Andrea Nierenberg, and you are...?"

Notice that most of these are "open-ended" questions, which require more than a one-word answer. The trick is to start the other person talking and to begin a conversation. When you've done your homework, you may even know something about the person you are meeting and be able to ask a pertinent question about his or her work or interests. This breaks the ice, and the conversation flows from there.

Have a List of "Get to Know You" Questions

Opening lines help you enter a conversation; get-to-know-you questions are different. They focus on the person you are speaking with, instead of the event or organization, and help you to develop a more personal relationship that helps your network grow.

AN UNUSUAL ICEBREAKER

My friend Barbara uses this unusual, yet effective icebreaker to kill two birds with one stone. When she meets someone and learns the person's name (Tom, in this case) she immediately says, "So nice to meet you, Tom." Then she uses his name again a few minutes later, as she talks about how hard it can be to remember names and how she has been working on this for some time. She reveals that one of the things she has learned is to repeat the name. She and Tom get into a conversation about remembering names and guess what? Not only has she broken the ice, she is also sure to remember Tom's name!

Two years ago I was in Europe to give a workshop and speech. As I entered the auditorium, there was a room full of people all staring at their notes or staring at me. They were early, so as I was setting up, I said, "Take this opportunity to get to know the people around you."

You would have thought I had asked them to give a State of the Union address! Everyone sat in silence. One woman finally said, "We don't do that here." I smiled and said, "We don't do it much where I'm from, either. However, go ahead and try it and see what happens. Remember why you came into this session on 'Networking to Build New Relationships.' Have some fun and remember, this room is almost like a laboratory class."

Knowing that people love to follow specific instructions, I asked them to turn to their neighbors and ask one or more of the following questions:

- Why did you come to this session?
- Where do you live?
- Where do you work and what do you do?
- How can someone tell when a company needs the services you or your company provide?
- What do you do when you're not working?
- What do you love about your work?
- What type of projects do you get involved in, and what have you done recently?
- What are some of the trends going on in your field?

At first, they just sat, and then about thirty seconds later they all started talking at once and kept at it. It was hard to get them to stop so I could start the session. When I finally got their attention again, I asked one of my favorite questions, "Who just met someone interesting?" Of course, every hand went up. Then I asked them to share a few things they had learned about each other. People discovered they had friends in common, grew up in the same neighborhoods, and had shared interests and hobbies. More important to their business lives, they met colleagues who could help with projects, they learned about parts of the company they had never known, and they discovered how they could become a resource for others.

Develop your own set of get-to-know-you questions using the ones above as a guide. Add questions relating to family, travel, hobbies, favorite books and movies, and the like. Add business-related questions appropriate to the situation. Use them at your next event, and I guarantee you'll meet someone interesting.

Develop a List of Idea-Generator Topics (Small Talk)

Some people are great at small talk. They seem to know something about many subjects and start a conversation on any of them. You can, too. Write ideas down as you think of them or read or hear something of interest to others. Become conversant about current affairs, best-selling books, movies, business news, the stock market, and certainly the latest news and trends in your own industry. Keep a journal of such topic ideas, organized by subject. Develop opening lines around topics that are current and in the news.

Every day the papers and news shows are filled with information that most people will know about. However, you have to be careful that your topic is not too controversial. Topics related to politics and sex are usually best addressed some time down the road. You don't really want to find yourself in disagreement with your new acquaintance. If this happens, gracefully move on to another topic that is a little less provocative.

The bonus for doing your small talk research is that you become knowledgeable and more well-rounded. People enjoy talking with people who are both interesting and knowledgeable. Small talk is also part of the exploration process in conversation that leads to discovering opportunities and common interests. As you feel more at ease with the art of small

A TIP ON WHERE TO FIND IDEA GENERATORS

Read the *Wall Street Journal* every day, either online or in print, and another national paper that you respect, such as *USA Today*. These are considered news sources, and so much of what they cover appeals to a wide variety of people. Most important, they're well written and cover many topics in addition to finance and business. You'll learn a lot. A quick read of page one in the *Wall Street Journal* will give you many idea generators. If you really want to stand out, read the industry paper or magazine that is related to the event you attend so you have current information about that industry. I like to prepare by reading as many of these as I can find online.

talk and learn how it helps you get to know another person, you'll find how effectively it opens the door to trust and rapport.

Develop a Thirty-Second Infomercial about Yourself

How may times have you been asked, "What do you do?" Hundreds, I'm sure. It's the most common question at a networking event and, for that matter, at many meetings and gatherings and one you must be prepared to answer in a clear, concise, enthusiastic, and memorable way. All in thirty seconds or less! Think of this as your personal mini-infomercial. Remember, first impressions count, and you have a limited time to make a good impression. Remember to work at making these short and punchy.

Not long ago, I was at the last table where the presenter wanted each attendee to introduce him or herself. Since so many people went before our group, it was a slow and painful process. I watched the glaze come over most peoples' eyes. So much time was spent on introductions, some lasting five minutes or more, that the speaker we all came to hear had to cut down his speech. So, when preparing your introduction, start by answering the following questions:

- How do I want to be remembered?
- What is the "headline" and benefit statement about you that will stand out in someone's mind?
- What is it about you that makes you unique compared to everyone else who does what you do?

If you merely state your job title and assume the other person will light up with excitement, it won't happen. That's because it may be easy, but it is not memorable to state only your title, position, or profession, such as, "I'm an investment advisor," "I'm vice president of sales," "I'm a computer consultant," or "I'm a real estate agent." Or, in my case, I might say, "I run a management consulting company." These statements actually tell the other person nothing about you and usually bring the conversation to a quick end.

When you want to make a more appealing introduction, consider these instead:

- "I help people retire early [send their kids to college, build their dream house]."
- "I coach salespeople on how to exceed their goals."
- "I make computers friendly."
- "I develop winning marketing campaigns."
- "I find people their dream home."
- "I assist people in developing their financial goals."

And, in my case, "I take the anxiety out of presentation and networking skills." The key to your response to the question, "What do you do?" is a statement that is memorable and will lead to further questions about you and your business (your thirty-second infomercial). Or in the case of my doctor, "I keep people breathing."

How to Test Your Personal Infomercial

Advertisers often test their commercials long before they go into production to see how effectively they communicate. You can do the same with your personal introduction; here's how to do just that:

- **Ask yourself, "Does my opening statement make the other person say, 'Tell me more!'"** Whatever your response to "What do you do?" or the opening of your thirty-second infomercial, make your statement leave the other person wanting to know more. Sometimes, when I open with, "I remove stage fright," and the response is, "How do you do that?" I then respond, "Workshops, consulting, and speaking engagements." Now I can develop and build the conversation depending on the interests of the other person. Often I am asked who attends or who books these workshops, seminars, and speaking engagements. This gives me an opportunity to describe my target audience. If the person I'm speaking with is the target, great. If not, maybe the person knows someone who is.

■ **Determine if you are specific enough.** Paint a word picture in the other person's mind. Remember that while we all meet so many people, it is important to make ourselves stand out. Otherwise, you'll be one in a sea of names that all end up underwater. Here are two examples—one bad and one good—of putting a picture in the mind of the other person:

■ <u>Hard to see:</u> "I am a nutritionist and create diet plans with supplements to help people lose weight."

■ <u>Easy to visualize:</u> "I help people get and stay in control of their eating patterns. I helped one women go from 250 pounds to a Britney Spears look-alike. One man had a forty-two-inch waist, and now thirty-four-size pants are loose on him."

POSITIONING YOURSELF

Positioning revolves around your core marketing message that should clearly state:

■ Who you are

■ Who you work with

■ What solutions you provide

■ What benefits you offer

■ What results you produce

■ What is special and unique about you

■ **Staying enthusiastic and upbeat are key.** Do you enjoy what you do, and does it show? When you're excited about your work or professional interests, you'll naturally come across as a passionate and energetic person. I have seen it so many times. Whatever your personality type (e.g., introverted, extroverted), you'll still come across as someone worth learning more about.

■ **What benefits and solutions to problems do you provide?** Always think of how you convey what you do as a benefit to the other person or a solution to a problem. I heard one person put it very well in communicating the problems she solves and the solutions: "I work with organizations that are facing the many challenges of a slow economy." Here's another one that works: "You know how many businesses struggle to find new customers? I have a service that guarantees them new business."

■ **Reflect on what makes you and your services unique.** We all should know enough about our markets to have distinguished ourselves from the competition. Part of your thirty-second infomercial should convey this information. It may be a process you use in your business, or a special type of client you service, or a brand-new product you offer. Be sure to communicate your uniqueness. Look at these examples:

Lawyer: "My firm works with zoning cases for churches, synagogues, and mosques. We've helped houses of worship buy property when it seemed impossible."

Image consultant: "I help people make 'million dollar' first impressions by showing how just one good hairstyle and three attractive outfits will make them more appealing to new clients."

CEO of a computer software company: "When small businesses think they can't afford powerful client management software, they call us. We help businesses, even with just a dozen employees, run like a Fortune 500 company."

Book publisher: "We publish business books for the busy executive. When someone wants best practices for customer service, she can read our books in the least time to get the best information."

Real estate agent: "First-time home buyers are anxious about their upcoming purchase. I take away all the pressure of finding properties within their budget so they can move in as soon as they want."

Set a Goal for Every Event or Meeting You Attend

Most managers know how to define realistic goals for their departments and plan strategies for meeting them. Before you attend any important meeting, especially if you are shy, set a realistic goal for that event, even if it is to establish contact with two people.

My friend, Jerry, used to stand in a corner at company meetings and other gatherings while people around him were greeting each other and getting into lively conversations. Although he is a highly respected executive, he suffered from severe shyness (familiar to many of us) that made him very uncomfortable in networking situations. Often he would attend these meetings with his associate, Nick, who was extremely gregarious and social. Jerry knew he had to make business contacts and he also desperately wanted to have more interactions. Attending these events with Nick put added pressure on Jerry because he thought he couldn't keep up with him.

"Begin slowly," I told him. "Set a goal before you leave the office to meet at least two new people. Plan on meeting just two new people with whom you will engage in conversation, ask some open-ended questions, and exchange pleasantries." I told him that he could meet more if he wanted, but he needed to keep in mind that the goal was at least two. And if Jerry felt there was a reason to meet again, I suggested that he send a note or e-mail or call to set up a follow-up meeting over breakfast or lunch. In any event, he should send both a short thank you for their time and conversation. (If he had his tangible networking kit handy with note cards, he'd be set.)

The key for Jerry and for you is to set a goal to make a specific number of quality connections (Jerry's goal was two) at every meeting, gathering, or event you attend. Two is a realistic goal for everyone. Think quality rather than quantity.

Arrival—Take a Deep Breath

You made it to the event. You did your research; you have opening lines, small talk topics, and have polished your thirty-second infomercial. Now it's showtime. You're ready!

Introduce Yourself to the Host

BE THE "APPROACHER" MORE OFTEN THAN AN "APPROACHEE"

Even if you are shy, take a risk and make it your goal to approach two people. In one of my workshop exercises to help people meet each other, I say, "Take two minutes and meet someone new. Ask the people who they are and where they work or, if they're in your company, what department and what comes to mind when they hear the word networking." I then ask everyone, "Who approached whom first?" Usually the people who were approached felt happy and complimented that someone chose them. I then say, "Use this technique and, at every event, you'll start to enjoy this part of networking." By being the approacher you'll be a better networker and you'll make others feel better and more comfortable.

Usually, one of the jobs of the host is to introduce people to each other, especially when new members or visitors are thinking of joining the group. You did your research and know whom to find in the crowd. Find the host or designated greeter and ask for help. Even better, drop this person a note in advance saying you are attending the meeting and hope he or she could help you meet several people. This shows your appreciation for the person's time and your enthusiasm for the event in advance. The host or greeter just might be ready for you when you arrive.

One night at an association event cocktail party, I lingered after checking in and, after reading the name tag on a woman at the registration desk, said, "Barbara, it's nice to meet you. I've read your organization's newsletter, and it sounds like you have a lot of active members. May I ask your help in introducing me to a couple of people here to break the ice?" She gladly took me around to several people with whom I was able to talk for the remainder of the evening. When I arrived at the next meeting, I was more comfortable and walked right over to reconnect with those I had met earlier. Of course, I followed up with a short note to thank Barbara for introducing me.

Get in Line

A great strategy for meeting people at the beginning of any event is to head for the bar, refreshment table, or registration desk—wherever there's a line. Most people are not fond of lines, but at events where you want to meet new people, lines provide a natural opportunity to start a conversation with the person in front or behind you. I actually like lines. Here's an example of how networking while standing in a line worked for me.

It was 11:45 in the morning, right before lunch, and there was a line in front of the ladies' room (where else) at the restaurant where I was attending a meeting. I noticed the name tag on the woman in front of me and realized we were attending the same meeting.

"Have you come to these meetings before?" I asked her. I also complimented her on the interesting necklace she was wearing. As we chatted, I learned she was vice president of marketing for a large New York newspaper. By the time we reached the beginning of the line, we had exchanged cards and I had promised that I would send her some information about my workshops and consulting business. Three months later, when she was planning a sales meeting, she contacted me and hired me to do a presentation at her event.

Now she has become a valued client—all because we started talking in the line for the ladies' room. Just be open and aware and realize an opportunity could be right in front of you.

Dive into a Group

Approaching a group of people engaged in active discussion is hard to do. Look for a group that looks friendly. They may be laughing, smiling, or enjoying each other's companionship. Wait for an opening, and say, "I don't mean to interrupt, but you seem like a friendly group. I'm new here. Would you mind if I joined you?" Who could say no to that? Often when I use this approach, people smile and say to me, "You have courage. I admire the fact that you can do this. It's nice to meet you." This is something I do a lot because I walk into many places where I am new and have to jump in.

I had just arrived in Los Angeles and was going to be speaking the next day to a group of anesthesiologists on presentation skills. That's right, I was going to be talking about speaker skills to a group that normally puts people to sleep. There was a cocktail party that evening, and as I walked into the room, everyone was engaged in conversation. I looked around and saw that most of the people were talking in pairs. I usually don't dive into conversation with two people who are talking together because it could be personal.

Then I spotted a group of three people smiling and chatting informally. I walked over and said, "I hope it's okay to join you. You seem so friendly." They were great, and I ended up talking with the main anesthesiologist for the session. By the time I spoke the next day, we were buddies. Take a risk and you may meet some very interesting people along the way.

Admittedly, approaching others already in a group is not easy. Even with all of your preparation it can still be uncomfortable. So, what I sometimes do is give myself a pep talk before approaching people I don't know. Think of positive and interesting things about yourself, such as:

- I'm glad to be here because it's going to help me grow professionally.
- I'm an expert in my field and eager to be a resource to others.
- I'm a great listener.
- I'm a friendly person and eager to learn and meet new people.

It's all in your attitude. Positive self-talk really works. I remember watching the Olympics and observing how top athletes give themselves a pep talk before their performance. If it works for them, it can work for you. However, be sure to give your pep talk silently.

NETWORKING GOES TO THE DOGS

I practice smiling and saying hello to people who are walking their dogs. People are generally friendly, and even if they aren't, their dogs usually are. Try this exercise if you are uncomfortable about approaching new people; it's good practice. Also, as you continue to see some of the same people, it's a way of getting to know them over time and perhaps making them a new contact.

Once, on a plane to Chicago, I was going over my notes for a speech. Part of my preparation is, of course, a pep talk. After I did my pep talk, I took off my earphones. As the plane descended, several people around me started to applaud. I had forgotten where I was, and everyone heard me talking to myself!

Start a Conversation with Your Dinner Partner

Look to your left. Look to your right. Your dinner partners could become important members of your network. At a seated meal, use your ice breaker opening lines and your idea generators and start the conversation rolling. As my dear friend, Jon, always says, business meals are certainly not about the food. They are about connecting and learning from others.

At a long event, you'll have opportunities to speak with more than just the people beside you. Here are a few suggestions to meet others besides those seated directly next to you:

- When there's a lull in the conversation, clink on a glass and suggest that the group introduce themselves to one another.
- Get up and walk around between courses to chat with other people at the table or around the room.
- Once everyone has finished eating, trade seats with the person next to you or with someone seated across from you, so you can get to know others at the table.

Of course, ask your dinner colleagues for permission to do this as a way for all of you to connect and meet several others . You don't want to insult anyone by moving around. People will probably be glad you were the one to take charge and create more interaction. You'll be the hero.

During the Event, Make a Connection and Plan to Follow Up

When you first meet someone at an event, your goal should be to make a connection and learn something about the person that will create reasons to follow up and begin to build a relationship. I discuss more about communication and connecting with others and then following up later. Until then, here are a few essential tips to use during a networking event.

Listen and Learn

My goal is to first learn about the other person before talking about myself. I want to learn something about the person so that I can be a resource to him or her. Networking is first about giving, and then you may get something back. As you are speaking and connecting with someone, pay specific attention to what the person is saying and what he or she doesn't say. Watch the person's body language and listen with both your ears and eyes.

My friend, Michelle, who is a financial adviser, told this story about communicating with various people in her network. She and another person at her firm were both engaged in supplying information to a client. The client was clearly an e-mail person and wanted information quickly. Michelle's colleague, Joe, wasn't an e-mail person and was not responding quickly enough with the information Michelle needed. When she questioned him, he said that he only checked e-mail once a day. This was a problem for Michelle as the customer needed speedy communication. The problem was solved when Joe then offered to give Michelle his assistant's name and e-mail. Joe's assistant replied quickly to Michelle's e-mails, and the client was happy.

We often meet people who prefer a different form of communication from the one we use. If we wish to build a relationship with them, we need to learn to be flexible. I know that I am almost always the service provider, so I always ask what the client wants and accommodate him or her.

Find Out Preferred Ways to Stay in Touch

Busy people know how they want to hear from others. When you meet someone you want to stay in contact with, be sure to ask, "What's the best way for us to keep in touch?" Everyone has a preferred method of communication. Some people like the telephone. Even if they can't take a call, voice mail works for them. I have carried on full conversations with people by exchanging voice mail messages.

Other people like e-mail, which is clearly the most popular form of business communication today, and are very good at responding quickly, as we all should be. I have one client who does not like e-mail. She knows she needs e-mail and it's the number one form of business communication, yet she isn't comfortable using it and isn't prompt in returning all the correspondence she receives. On the other hand, as soon as she receives a phone call, she responds immediately. Therefore, I know exactly how to communicate with her. In my network database I have a "V" for voice mail next to her name. Another man I know rarely returns a call. He even told me, "I don't like the telephone!" I clearly know how to communicate with him. He does return his e-mails, so I put an "E" for e-mail next to his name in my contact list. You might be thinking, "This is weird." Maybe, but people all have unique ways of staying in touch and conducting business. As a service provider who wants to connect with them, we need to learn to follow suit.

The important thing is to ask your contact about his or her preference and make a note of it, either mentally or on the small notepad in your tool kit, and then enter it into your database so you'll always remember to use it when following up and keeping in touch.

Have an Exit Strategy

When you have a room full of people to meet, or even your designated two, it's a good idea to make sure that you don't monopolize people's time. (They most likely also have goals for people they want to meet.) Even when you're engrossed in a great conversation, it is perfectly polite to leave something for next time and close your conversation with a follow-up suggestion.

The other scenario that calls for an exit strategy is when you're talking with someone and you find yourself mentally counting the minutes until you can get away. Whatever the situation, you need some conversation enders and ways to wrap it up with grace and style. Here are some that work well:

- "It was great meeting you, and I hope we can continue our conversation sometime over lunch or coffee."
- "Thanks for sharing the information about your new project. It sounds exciting. Best of continued success."
- "Please excuse me, I see a friend I'd like to go over and visit with. Enjoy your evening."
- "I enjoyed hearing about your company and look forward to seeing you again."
- "Let me introduce you to_____. He may be a good person to discuss some of the challenges you are facing."
- "I'm so glad we met. Lots of good luck, and if I hear of anything that might be a fit for you, I'll definitely be in touch."

"SORRY I CAN'T TALK TO YOU, I'M HERE TO NETWORK"

I had just walked into an evening event with my friend, Bruce, when we ran into a woman whom Bruce knew. She looked at us both and, without saying hello, announced, "Sorry, I can't talk to you. I'm here to network!"

How sad for her. She was only out for herself and trying much too hard to get something, certainly without giving first. Not to mention the fact that she made her friend Bruce feel like chopped liver.

She could have spent a few minutes chatting before disengaging to meet new people. Networking is not always about making new contacts; it's also about nurturing your current contacts. In fact, reconnecting with some of your contacts and clients can be a real goal for an event. Besides, it's nice to visit with old friends, get back on their radar, and create a stronger relationship.

Before I start my exit, I always ask for a card. I know that I will follow up with at least a short note and perhaps a phone call for a meeting. I usually wait until people ask me for my card instead of just giving them one of mine. Remember, I asked for their card first because I was interested and knew I would follow up. Over time, when we continue to build rapport, they will learn all about me.

We've walked through the entire networking event, from research and goal-setting to your exit strategy. Make sure you arrive ready and, once you're there, dive in and accomplish your goals. We've also touched on the importance of listening. In the following chapter, we take that skill to the next level: discovering a process that will take ordinary conversations and transform them into extraordinary discoveries to help benefit your business life.

What's the Point of Techniques for Networking Success?

Success at networking functions doesn't come naturally for most of us; it requires some planning and preparation. Without it, your network is unlikely to grow. With it, you'll succeed far beyond your expectations, regardless of your previous networking experience.

Exercise 1—Setting Goals

List five goals that will help you be more successful when attending an event with a large number of people you have never met.

1._____

2._____

3._____

4._____

5._____

Write down what event(s) you need to attend in the next month and up to two goals that you have for each event.

Name of event:_____

Goal(s):_____

_____

Name of event:_____

Goal(s):_____

_____

Name of event:_____

Goal(s):_____

_____

Exercise 2—Meeting People in Line

List five places where you can meet people standing in line.

1._____

2._____

3._____

4._____

5._____

Exercise 3—Use Your Thirty-Second Infomercial in Different Situations

Throughout the year, you may experience one or more of the following situations in which you will want to use your thirty-second infomercial. Although your information is the same, you may want to position yourself a little differently in each situation. Take a look at these situations and tailor your infomercial to address your audience.

1. Networking event
2. Company party
3. Business-related volunteer group
4. Chamber of commerce meeting
5. Seminar
6. Charity event
7. Neighborhood association meeting

Exercise 4—Opening Lines

Opening lines are important for connecting with people. Write an opening line for each of the following situations:

1. At a holiday party, you are meeting someone from your company whom you did not know.

_____

_____

_____

2. While on a plane, you want to start a conversation with the person sitting next to you.

_____

_____

_____

3. While riding on an elevator, you realize that a key business contact you want to know, and with whom you have never spoken, is standing right next to you.

_____

_____

_____

_____

4. You are standing in a buffet line and you overhear some people talking about something you're interested in.

_____

_____

_____

5. You meet some people on vacation while on a tour.

_____

_____

_____

"No person will make a great business who wants to do it himself or get all the credit."
—Andrew Carnegie

"If you think you are too small to be effective, you have never been in bed with a mosquito."
—Anita Roddick

GROW:
Building on
Your Strengths

"God gives every bird its food, but He does not throw it into the nest."

—J.C.Holland

Once you have found the key relationships in your business life and know the tools for continuing to find them, you must then grow the business and relationships to keep them prospering.

In this section, we address the skills and tactics to do just that. You will start to enhance your listening skills and other key communication skills to use every day of your life so that you can become the ultimate professional. You will discover the secrets to communicating and working with all of the personality types, easily and with minimum effort. You will also find out ways to positively create your own "self brand" so that you will be able to market yourself in a seamless way. We will discuss the advantage of the quiet or introverted networking style in depth, and finally move into the key components for effective follow up.

This section is chock full of information and materials that you can put to use immediately.

CHAPTER 4

Listening and Learning

> *"If I listen, I have the advantage. If I speak, others have it."*
>
> **—Arabic proverb**

Two men were walking down a busy New York City street one day when, above the noise of the cars, trucks, and honking horns, one said to the other, "Listen to that cricket." His companion replied, "How can you hear a cricket in the middle of all of this noise?" Without saying a word, the first man took a coin from his pocket, flipped it in the air, and let it bounce on the sidewalk with its familiar metallic sound. A dozen heads turned and feverishly looked for the bouncing coin. "We hear what we listen for," the first man sagely remarked.

I love this story and often use it to illustrate the importance of good communication skills—especially listening—in making contacts and building relationships. The first step in building trust and respect with your new contacts and your current network is to listen and learn. This requires good communication skills, effective listening, and the ability to recognize and honor different communication styles and personality types.

Communication Skills for the Effective Networker

Once you've mastered the techniques for meeting people and gained more confidence, you are ready to master the communication skills that will help you connect with those you want in your network. It's all about building rapport and learning how to interact with ease. Many of you know these skills and already use them to the utmost. Consider this a reminder as you put them into action.

Start with a Smile

Everyone responds well to a smile. When you meet someone, it's the most important thing you can wear. It's also the first step in building rapport. Remember to smile when you enter a room, begin a business meeting, and answer the phone. When you smile, the other person becomes the mirror that reflects your expression. A smile can raise your spirits and even affect the way you sound.

For telephone encounters, I give people mirrors with the phrase printed on the case, "Can your smile be heard?" I tell them to put the mirror on their desk when they are talking on the phone to see their expressions. And, yes, a smile can be heard. I always remember what my dear friend, Florence, used to say before picking up the telephone—"Have a smile on your face and visualize the words *opportunity* and *decorum*." It's amazing how doing this will change your inner perception.

I know some of you may be rolling your eyes thinking, "How can I keep a mirror on my desk? My colleagues will think I'm vain." Don't worry, I've seen mirrors on the desks of many very successful people, who are merely checking out their presentation image when they're on the phone.

Remember that a smile can disarm another person. Your face speaks volumes and encourages people either to open up to you or to walk away. It is a powerful tool to use when meeting new people in a networking situation, so use it to your advantage. I make it a habit to walk into every meeting, event, or encounter with a smile on my face. I also have gotten into the habit of smiling at three new people every day. It's warm and refreshing and totally diffuses any tension. Remember to be discreet, however. I live in New York City, so I advise people not to walk down the street grinning. I'm talking about sincere, feel-good hello—and nothing else—smiles.

> *"The deeds you do today may be the only sermon some people will hear today."*
> **—St. Francis of Assisi**

Look the Other Person in the Eye

Have you ever been talking with a person who was looking over your shoulder instead of at you? Did you think to yourself, "He doesn't think I'm important" or "She's not even listening to me"? Making good eye contact shows respect and interest and it's good manners.

At a casual networking event, Carol, a vice president of human resources for a large financial services company, and her assistant, Barbara, talked to a vendor. During the entire conversation, Bill, the vendor, never looked at Barbara. He focused totally on her boss, Carol, who he thought was the sole decision maker. As it turned out, it was actually Barbara who made the purchasing decisions for Bill's services! He paid no attention to her and, when it came time to order, she gave her business to another vendor with comparable services, but better manners.

Eye contact is one of the strongest communication skills we can develop. It's been said, and I believe it's true, "The eyes are the windows to the soul."

Another time I was at an event where a man started talking with me because I had just been on a panel. During our conversation, he kept looking past my left shoulder. At first I thought I had something hanging from it or a stain. Then, in mid-sentence, he left me standing and seemed to fly over to talk with someone else. I thought it was rude, yet these things happen. It was ironic that, as I was walking to get a soda, I heard my name called out, and a friend motioned me for me to join him. As I walked over, I saw my "former acquaintance" (the one who had left me to talk with someone he thought he could sell something to). Little did he know that "someone" happened to be my friend. I can still see him squirming when my friend said, "Have you two met?" I smiled, and somehow Mr. Rude decided to take a more proper exit strategy with no immediate sales. Again—you never know!

MAKING EYE CONTACT

Fifty-five percent of communication is visual. When you neglect to make eye contact, you may be communicating that you are uninterested, bored, or, worse yet, sneaky and untrustworthy! In reality, it may be because you are shy or nervous about attending the event. If you find eye contact challenging, practice making eye contact with yourself in the mirror while you're on the phone. When you're in front of someone and can't look into his or her eyes, try to focus somewhere around the eyes between the nose and forehead. I call this area the "third eye." Soon it will become easier for you.

Remember Names

Dale Carnegie, author of *How to Win Friends and Influence People*, wrote, "A person's name is to him or her the sweetest and most important sound in any language." So it really pays to remember names, because people know you have heard what they've said. Here are three ways to sharpen your name-recall skills:

1. Form an impression of the person's appearance and embed it into your mind. Note height, stature, color of hair and eyes, facial expression, and any distinguishing physical features. I always remember my late friend, Fred White, who had the whitest hair you ever saw. His name was easy to remember! Don't concentrate so much on dress, or even hairstyle. These may be different the next time you meet. (I'm the perfect example! How many of you read *Nonstop Networking* and saw me with different hair? It always changes!) Concentrate on remembering the person's face.

2. Repeat the person's name after you meet and a couple of times during the conversation. When you repeat the name, two things happen: First, you make your contact feel good, and, second, the name goes into your memory bank. Often when I teach, I meet so many people with very unusual and wonderful names. I always ask them to repeat their names so I pronounce them correctly. Then I use it several times. However, be sure not to turn it into a distraction and use the name too often in a short conversation. The best policy is to repeat it at the beginning when the person first says it, in the middle, and again at the end when you are exiting.

3. Make up a visual story about the person's name. Associate the person's name with something that will remind you of it. Use your imagination and paint a story in your mind. Put the person into your visual story. The sillier the story, the easier it will be to remember. For example, I met someone in one of my workshops, named George Whitehouse. I

remembered his name by picturing him standing in front of the presidential White House, and he was shaking hands with none other than our first president, George Washington. Hence my new contact—George Whitehouse—and an attorney at that! At your next meeting, take time to practice this with several new people you meet.

4. Also write down the names of people as they walk into a meeting and write a word or two describing them to jog your memory. I always do this when I'm speaking or training and want to remember the names of people in my audience so I can address them personally. With effort and practice, you can remember anyone's name.

You Are a Star (whatever you name is...)

NOTE TO BRAIN:

Delete this phrase: "I'm not good at remembering names."

Replace it with: "I'm getting better at remembering names all the time."

Whatever you tell your brain is a self-fulfilling prophecy.

Once I was working for a company and had the opportunity to speak with its president at a luncheon meeting. He was in the business of personalized stationary and prided himself on remembering names. You can imagine my surprise when I received a beautiful card from him a few weeks later. On the front it said, "You are a Star." The inside note started with, "Dear Angela" (oops).

"You are what you repeatedly do. Excellence is not an event—it is a habit."

—Aristotle

Introduce and Reintroduce Yourself

"Oh, my gosh! I hope he doesn't see me!" It's that awful feeling that comes over you when you see someone whose name you should remember, but your brain has just turned off. There's no need to panic. Chances are, if you draw a blank on the name of someone you've met before, that person may not remember your name, either. Simply put out your hand as I do and say, "Hi, I'm Andrea Nierenberg. We met at the last meeting." (Of course, use your own name!) Most people reciprocate happily and reintroduce themselves. If not, just ask, "Please tell me your name again" or "Refresh my memory. What is your name again?" or "Forgive me, please tell me your name again." I then repeat it aloud and then repeat it silently several times and make a mental note to remember it.

It is also a good practice to reintroduce yourself to those you may have just met. While you may remember their names and use them, they may have forgotten yours and they will appreciate your gesture.

Be Aware of Your Body Language

A friend of mine always scratches her head when faced with something unpleasant. We may not realize we have these habits, so it pays to become aware of them because they convey a less-than-positive body image. Avoid nervous habits such as blinking eyes, licking lips, fidgeting, twirling a strand of hair, stroking your mustache, or drumming your fingers. Remember Ralph Waldo Emerson's wise words: "What you do speaks so loudly that I cannot hear what you say."

You can say a lot without opening your mouth. Research tells us that we form perceptions in three ways: Verbal makes up 7 percent, non-verbal is 38 percent, and visual is 55 percent of our perception of others.

Notice that body language makes up the biggest percentage. Make sure your body language communicates what you truly want to say. This is why the phrase, "actions speak louder than words," is so true.

Practice good posture. Standing tall and straight reflects confidence. Be aware of your facial expression. Your expression says a lot before you even open your mouth. Remember to look relaxed and happy to meet the person. Use good eye contact, smile, and react to the conversation with appropriate nonverbal actions such as nodding and showing encouragement and interest. You might want to ask a trusted adviser or friend if you have or do anything that could take away from creating a stellar impression. My sister, Meredith, has helped me a lot here. I remember her asking me, "Do you realize that you say 'really' a lot? In fact, once I counted twenty-seven times during a conversation!" At first, I was taken aback and then I realized, "Wow, she's right!" I've become so aware of this and other pet phrases that can take away from my presentation. Meredith is a great help and she certainly tells it like it is!

Your handshake is also part of your body language. A soft and floppy grip may imply that you lack confidence or are unenthusiastic, whereas a vice-like grip may imply that you are overly forceful and aggressive.

Robert E. Brown and Dorothea Johnson offer this sage advice in their book, *The Power of Handshaking*: "Handshakes reveal inner traits, personality, and motivations. The hands can't conceal messages as the spoken word can. Your hands are messengers of your subconscious mind, and whether you like it or not, your handshake will often betray your emotional state."

They are very right. You want to appear self-confident and friendly and open to your new contact. Here are some tips for a proper handshake:

1. Grip the other person's hand firmly at the point where the webs of your thumbs meet.

2. Shake from the elbow, not the shoulder, and just a couple of times.

3. Hold for only a few seconds and end cleanly.

4. Use only one hand. Don't use your other hand to cover the other person's hand.

Brown and Johnson call this the all-American handshake: "This is the handshake delivered by corporate executives and champions of both genders. This person makes eye contact, smiles, offers a firm grip, and two or three firm strokes. The handshake delivers a feeling of relaxed self-confidence. This is a warm and genuine greeting acceptable worldwide."

Just as important as a firm, friendly handshake are these other gestures that reveal your readiness to meet new people:

B—Breathe deeply and consistently. This steadies your nerves and gives you a pleasant facial expression that says, "I'm glad to be speaking with you."

O—Overtures can speak volumes. Nod to show encouragement and that you are listening. Keep an open posture to show you are receptive.

D—Demeanor is the part of your personality demonstrated by body language. A blank stare, crossed arms, nervous gestures, all convey the opposite of what you want to communicate.

Y—"You," means, "I am focused on you." Observe how others interact and find a way to match it. For example, if you're sitting across the table from a person who is leaning in to create a closer connection, follow suit. If you lean back, this could say to him or her, "I'm not interested."

Be Respectful of Others' Boundaries

The invisible boundaries around us that define our personal space vary from culture to culture. Most Americans become uncomfortable when someone is closer than eighteen inches. In some countries, standing as close as we do in the United States is considered too far apart. In other places, it's too close. People's boundaries are not only an issue for travelers. America is a melting pot, so we need to be aware of the diversity within our own country.

Brown and Johnson advise: "Watch how far an individual extends the arm to shake your hand. As a general rule, the straighter the arm, the more protective he or she is of personal space."

Look for Common Interests

Ask open-ended questions like those you developed in the previous chapter and listen to what others say in response. Practice your list of get-to-know you questions, so they are easy and come automatically. Phrase them so they can't be answered with a single word. And be sure to have a follow-up question ready.

Some people you meet will take your questions quite literally. "Did you enjoy the speaker?" you ask, hoping to start a conversation. "Yes" is the answer you get, followed by silence. So change your question to, "How did you find the speaker's presentation?" You may still get, "Fine." Then you can follow with, "What did you particularly like about it?" or "What did you think of his message?"

Once you establish your common interests, the conversation will begin to flow, and you will find reasons to follow up and keep in touch. For example, you may be able to say, "I have an article you might enjoy based on what the presenter talked about. May I send you a copy?"

Give Genuine Compliments

When you listen to people carefully, often they will mention something about which they are proud. Think for a moment and find a way to acknowledge their achievement. Make a goal of finding at least one positive trait or characteristic in each person you meet that you can compliment. It may seem awkward at first, but it will soon become second nature.

It could even be something small. For example, I think one great accessory is a good pen. In fact, I often give nice pens to my best business contacts as premiums, **without** my name on them. I think they're classier if they're plain. I was at a meeting once and saw a woman with a beautiful pen in her hand and commented how much I liked it. This simple compliment on her taste in writing utensils started the conversation rolling and eventually, as we got to know each other, we found we had other, very similar preferences. I practice this continually; it's both fun and empowering and it makes the other person feel good.

I think back to a woman I used to work with early in my career. She was never one to mince words and sometimes they would come out as less than encouraging. I remember saying to her over lunch, "You have taught me a lot with your direct, no-nonsense approach to things. I know that sometimes people don't understand you—however, I do and I thank you for who you are."

As a general rule, most of us don't give out compliments as often as they may be deserved. We worry that we'll come across as phony or as if we're doing it because we want something. This is why it is so important to be sincere and to give a compliment only when you mean it. Only then will it be truly meaningful to the recipient.

Sometimes you may give someone a compliment, and the recipient will not know how to receive it. This is a common reaction, and it shouldn't stop you. We all like to get a sincere compliment, even if some of us have a hard time showing our appreciation. I have also found that some people prefer public praise and others prefer private. When I ask in my workshops about people's preferences in this regard, there is always much discussion. When I ask for a show of hands, it seems most people don't mind public praise. However, there are some who just don't want to be the center of attention, even if it's really good attention. They are most comfortable in a support role. Most likely they will not tell you that they would rather not be praised publicly, so if you sense that this might be the case, don't be afraid to ask. Then simply tell the person at an opportune time what he or she did well or how it impressed you. Also, a thank-you card can mean the world to someone who prefers private praise. Take the time to observe and find out how people like to receive compliments and honor their preferences.

Right now, think of something you admire about some of your co-workers or other colleagues. Take a few minutes to jot down your thoughts and share them either verbally or in a note. Make a practice of doing this frequently and sincerely.

FIVE-A-DAY

Look for positive attributes in the people you come in contact with during the course of your day and compliment them. Make a goal to give "five a day." Put five pennies in your left-hand pocket in the morning. Each time you give a sincere compliment, take out a penny and put it into your right-hand pocket. By the end of the day, you should have transferred all five pennies. And you will have made at least five people feel good!

Talk Less, Listen More

One of the greatest compliments you can give another person is to let him or her know that you are listening to everything said. As Emerson said, "It is a luxury to be understood." Find the hidden word in *listen* using all the letters. The word is *silent*. That is what our internal voice must be to get the full impact of what others are saying. Remember that when you are networking with a new contact, it's like reading the paper. Let the person tell you his or her story so you can discover the "news you can use."

More people have literally talked themselves out of a job or a sale by speaking instead of sitting back and actively listening. It takes real concentration to listen. I read once that we only hear half of what is said to us, understand only half of that, believe only half of that, and remember only half of that.

Good salespeople have learned to listen first, then tailor their sales presentation to their potential clients' needs as presented in the first few minutes of conversation. The same holds true for meeting new people. They'll know you are genuinely interested in them as a person if you can "tailor" your comments to what they have just told you about themselves. Relate your experiences to theirs. For instance, often I will say, "That reminds me of…," based on what I just heard. When one participant in a workshop told me how she often got nervous before speaking in front of a group because she felt her heart beating so fast, I said, "I totally understand. That reminds me of when I was a young girl and would have to speak in front of my class for a report. I would remember my heart beating so fast, I thought everyone could hear it."

I also told her what someone told me ages ago: "No one can hear it beating, and just be glad it is!"

Are You an Effective Listener?

I recall a friend telling me this story about a dinner party she had attended. She was seated next to the guest of honor, a very distinguished older gentleman. After the meal, the host relayed a compliment to her from her dinner partner, "He thought you were the most fascinating person he met!" She told me she had hardly said a word all evening to this man. "He was so interesting. I just listened." Well, I know this woman very well. She is a fascinating woman, successful in her profession, and a very effective networker. She knows that if you sit back and listen, people will tell you a lot about themselves, how they like to communicate, and what is important to them. It's a great communication strategy and tool.

Good networkers, like my friend, take what they have learned to the next step, making a real connection with people they can help and who can help them. As we build on our networking and realize the skills we need to find, grow, and keep our business, one of the most critical skills we must develop is the ability to listen and to find ways to make a connection.

How Do You Rate as a Good Listener?

Consciously using active listening skills is a must. Rate yourself on a scale of 1 to 5 on these essential listening skills. Give yourself a 5 if, "I always do this with ease and confidence," and 1 if, "I rarely do this and feel awkward when I do."

1. I make eye contact. I always look the other person in the eye during our conversation and focus my full attention on him or her.

2. I ask questions for clarification. If I don't understand or need further clarification, I ask the other person to explain so that I can understand better. I restate what I think I understand, and then ask to make sure that is the intended meaning. For example, "What I'm hearing you say is…" or "Am I correct in understanding what you said is . . ."

3. I show concern by acknowledging feelings. I also listen with my eyes. I use positive body language by nodding and smiling when appropriate. I am empathetic.

4. I try to understand the speaker's point of view before giving mine. I recognize that the other person is far more interested in stating his or her point of view than in hearing mine. I also realize that my understanding of the other person's point of view leads to building a better relationship and a better response on my part.

5. I am poised and emotionally controlled. I hold back from jumping to conclusions or interrupting with what I want to say when the other person is speaking.

6. I react nonverbally with a smile or a nod. I know this shows my interest and allows the person to continue without interruption.

7. I pay close attention and do not let my mind wander. I am careful not to allow my mind to take a mental excursion. I concentrate on what the other party is saying rather than on formulating what I'm going to say next.

8. I avoid interrupting. Someone once gave me a great sign: "The most successful people have teeth marks on their tongue." Don't interrupt—let the other person finish. (This one can be tough—count how many times you interrupt someone or, easier, count how many times someone interrupts you and how it makes you feel.)

9. I avoid changing the subject without warning. I make sure the conversation on one subject is closed before jumping to the next subject. Changing the subject abruptly relays that you are not listening and only want to talk about whatever is on your mind.

How did you do?

If you scored 35–45, you're an exceptional listener.

If you scored 25–34, you're a very good listener.

If you scored 20–24, you're an average listener.

If you scored 15–19, keep working; you'll improve!

Take a good look at the areas where your rating could improve. Start to work on these, while continuing to practice the skills you've already mastered consistently. Take the test again in two weeks. Watch how your ratings improve when you commit to improving your listening skills.

Listening Skills Pay Off

Effective listening skills are not only critical to understanding and building relationships, they also pay off in business. I once asked the president of a company if he ever measured how much business his firm lost because someone didn't listen. He told me that the company once lost a million-dollar sale that he thought would be a sure thing. Two salespeople were

ARE YOU ALL EARS?

How would the following people in your life rate you as a listener?

■ Your best friend

■ Your boss

■ Your spouse or partner

■ Your best client(s)

■ Your employee(s)

■ Your dinner partner at the last party you attended

■ Someone who is challenging to listen to (this is a tough one)

Rate each on a scale of 1 to 5 with 5 being the best. Add the scores, then imagine your score on a continuum. On the very left, representing the lowest number, is a brick wall; on the right, representing the highest score, is a field of corn. Are you stuck up against the brick wall, or are you "all ears" in a field of corn?

involved in a conference call with the customer to close the deal. One didn't hear an important piece of information from the customer, and although the other one heard it, he misinterpreted its significance. The result was a lost sale.

The incidents and situations differ, yet the impact is the same: in most cases, when someone fails to listen and learn, the costs associated are extraordinary—in time, relationships, productivity, and money!

Interact with Ease

Think of someone you know who seems totally at ease mingling at business and social functions. What are the person's characteristics and behavior patterns? I often ask this of participants at my seminars and workshops. Based on the answers from hundreds of them through the years, here are ten common characteristics of people who interact with others with ease and grace:

1. They are able to make others feel comfortable.

2. They appear confident and at ease.

3. They are able to laugh at themselves—not at others.

4. They show interest in others by maintaining eye contact, self-disclosing, asking questions, and actively listening.

5. They extend themselves to others—lean into a greeting with a firm handshake and a smile.

6. They convey a sense of enthusiasm and energy.

7. They are well rounded, well informed, well intentioned, and well mannered.

8. They know vignettes or stories of actual events that are interesting, humorous, and appropriate.

9. They introduce people to each other with an infectious enthusiasm that inspires conversation.

10. They convey respect and genuinely like people.

People at my seminars and workshops who know or observe others with these characteristics and who possess some themselves tell me they are successful at their business; have a wide and effective network of friends, associates, and contacts; and tend to achieve their goals.

Communication Styles and Personality Types

Effective networkers are aware of communication styles and personality types. They know their own style, with its strengths and weaknesses, and they have learned to recognize and honor other people's styles of communication and personality types. They also adapt their style to accommodate others when appropriate.

What Is Your Communication Style?

Sometimes trying to communicate with someone who communicates differently from the way we do is like two ships passing in the night. We don't understand them, and they don't understand us.

To communicate effectively, be ready to alter the way you communicate. Once I was in France and was trying to communicate with a shopkeeper. I thought that if I spoke louder and more slowly in English, she would understand me. Of course, there was no way she could. The louder and more slowly I talked, the more frustrating it was for both of us. I needed to alter my style (talking at a regular volume in English) and try something else she could understand, such as pointing and gesturing, smiling, or even finding someone who could interpret for us (which I eventually did).

The frustration I felt before I altered my style is exactly the same feeling we have when we don't connect with someone else. We may be in our own country and speaking the same language, yet our communication styles are so different that we have a hard time making a connection. We need to understand and adapt our style to communicate effectively. I am a bottom-line person. Often I see the big picture first and then find a way to go for it, sometimes without thinking it totally through.

My publicist, Tom, on the other hand, is a process person. He looks at every detail, weighs both the positive and negative, and really thinks it through. Another fellow who is terrific and works with Tom is Duane, who is even more of a process person! I love them both and can now communicate with them so much better. I take the time to listen and hear every word and suggestion they give me and I learn along the way. There were times in the past, though, when I know we've all gotten frustrated because we only wanted to communicate "our" way. However, when we adapt, we do see things from the other person's point of view and we can work together much more clearly and effectively. At your next meeting or networking event, practice altering your style with each person you meet or connect with. In the course of a day or event, you will most likely find yourself changing your communication style with everyone you encounter.

Everyone uses a style of communication when giving and receiving information. Harry is auditory—he learns by hearing information. He rarely takes notes at a meeting and prefers a verbal briefing to a written report. He has told me that he listens to the news every morning and night, rather than reading a newspaper. When I speak with Harry, the auditory type, I am sure to incorporate phrases such as "Are we in harmony?" or "How does this sound to you?" I recognize that he will remember things he hears rather than sees, so I leave him voice mail messages rather than e-mail reminders.

Ann is visual—she needs to see pictures or "to see in it writing." She takes many notes in a meeting and treasures handouts and written reports. She loves PowerPoint presentations and flip charts. When she communicates, she often draws what she's talking about on a pad. When I talk with her, I say things like, "How does this look to you?" or "Picture this...." I know I need to paint a picture for Ann.

Bill is kinesthetic—he needs to act things out, be involved, or have things demonstrated to him. He talks with his hands or explains how to do something with a demonstration. He learns things best by actually doing them. With Bill, I say, "Are you comfortable with this idea?" or "How does this feel to you?"

Think about how you like to give and get information. What is your preferred communication style? What is that of your boss, various co-workers, your subordinates, even your spouse? Have you ever been frustrated trying to communicate something when the other person just didn't get it? Maybe your communication styles were too disparate. Think about how you could adapt your style to accommodate the other person's. Keep in mind, people won't tell you their style. You'll learn their preferred methods only by observation and careful listening. Hear the words they use and watch their behavior. Then you can match your words to theirs to communicate with them effectively.

Being a good listener and an effective communicator are keys to listening and learning. When you hear someone say, "This doesn't sound right to me," an effective response is, "What exactly are you hearing to make you say that?"

EACH COMMUNICATION STYLE HAS ITS OWN LANGUAGE

Visual	Auditory	Kinesthetic
See	Hear	Feel
Look	Listen	Touch
Picture	Sound	Emotion
Appear	Discuss	Aware

Dominant:

Bottom line-oriented, competitive, direct

Makes decisions quickly

Best approach to use:

- Focus on the "what"
- Be efficient

Influencer:

Persuasive, animated, expressive, emotional

Enjoys helping others

Best approach to use:

- Focus on the "who"
- Be empathetic

Steady:

Patient, agreeable, amiable, quiet

Is very dependable

Best approach to use:

- Focus on the "how"
- Be supportive

Conscientious:

Compliant, cautious, accurate, analytical

Likes lots of details

Best approach to use:

- Focus on the "why"
- Be logical

Recognizing Personality Types

In addition to being aware of communication styles, a good communicator adjusts to other people's orientation or personality type. Some people are more oriented, or sensitive, to the concerns and feelings of others; others are more bottom-line- or results-oriented. Still others are interested in and concerned with details and the way things work.

There are ways to identify personality and temperament traits that help predict how people react and relate to each other. One very popular personality style indicator used by many companies is the Myers-Briggs Type Indicator. I also use the DISC® profile, which explores behavioral issues. It has been around for more than thirty years and is an effective tool for understanding personality traits and styles. It is worth researching these and other personality indicators. However, for you to be effective, all you really need to do is listen carefully, observe behaviors, and then respect others' personality orientation. I have found that this works time and time again. Still, it takes practice.

For example, I once walked into a corporate conference room and found myself giving three different presentations at the same time! I was there to present a training proposal to three top decision makers in the company. Having met them all and through careful observation and listening, I knew each had a very different personality style. My main goal (besides selling my program) was to speak to their needs and convey the benefits to each one. Therefore, I needed to adjust my presentation to each one individually. As I spoke with each, I switched the way I conveyed the information I was giving to match his or her personality.

The head of human resources and training was amiable in her approach. What I remembered most about her was her comment to me about being sure to "get everyone involved" and her obvious caring and concern for all the employees. Clearly, I had to focus my presentation to her on the personal benefits for her employees and make sure she felt that the time her employees spent in training would be worthwhile for their growth and development.

The chief financial officer, however, was interested in the return on investment he expected from my program. In addition, he wanted details and numbers. I decided to give him the same proposal that I had given to the head of human resources but to include a specific outline for each module, with costs clearly defined. The more data I presented to him, the better!

The CEO told me he had only six minutes to hear me out. (I actually clocked how long he was in the room, and it was exactly six minutes!) All he wanted to know was, "What are my people going to learn?" and "How much will it cost?" I was prepared with the same presentation (in case he had questions), but I gave him only the executive summary: a brief, succinct paragraph followed by bullet points and the bottom line.

These were three very different people—all wanting the same thing yet needing it delivered in three very different ways. To succeed, I had to read each person carefully and provide him or her with exactly what that person wanted to hear.

Later, after I had done several programs with this firm, each person told me separately how much he or she enjoyed our working relationship because, "We communicate in exactly the same way." I smiled to myself, knowing that my extra work and effort to understand each personality type was well worth it!

Not a Chameleon

An effective networker is an excellent listener who understands and adapts to the needs of others. Be aware, however, that this does not mean constantly changing your personality. Nor does it mean being solicitous or manipulative. It is a positive, sincere, and proactive approach to understanding another's feelings and interests. You want to appear empathetic not opportunistic. Empathy means understanding someone else's feelings, thoughts, and experience without openly communicating that you do. Therefore, to become empathetic, just be aware of communication styles and personality types.

Men and Women: Do We Network Differently?

If personality types were the only thing that made us different, that would make communication challenging enough! Take all of these different types and mix in the fact that men and women perceive the world much differently. Now you have a real challenge! That's right—in our diverse world we need to take a good look at how being male or female affects how we listen and learn from one another.

Female vs. Male Bonding

First, let's look at how the sexes relate with members of the same gender. When we see what requirements men have to feel good about their communication with each other, and when we look at how women bond with each other, we can understand what we might do to communicate better with the opposite gender. These are generalities and are only useful in providing a framework of understanding. As helpful as these may be, there is no substitute for really getting to know other people and their communication preferences. The biggest difference to remember about understanding how women communicate with each other is that women bond more easily than men do, and in a different way.

One male client of mine heard his wife yell with sympathy on the phone one night. When he rushed into the room to ask her what happened, she said with tears that someone had stood up her friend on a date. He looked at her with disbelief, thinking that something life-threatening had happened! If this had been a male friend of his who had a woman cancel a date (if his friend would even tell him about it), his response would have been, "That's a bummer—want to come over and watch the game?"

In one accounting firm I work with, the women partners often try to give business to other women. We bond—often by the time coffee is served, we know the other woman's life story…and then we turn to business. We like to help each other once we have developed some trust.

Men tend to have some brief small talk and then dive right into doing business. They tend to think: "Why spend all that time getting to know each other, unless I know this will be a good business proposition? After the deal is done, then we can get to know each other. That will help us since we'll be working together. If all goes well on the business end of things, and there is some mutual respect, then we might recommend each other to our associates for further business opportunities." This is what I hear from my male counterparts—I can't vouch for it firsthand!

As you interact with the opposite sex, keeping these ideas in the back of your mind will help when you deal with any "speed bumps" in your communication. When communication is hard or breaks down between men and women, more often than not it's because we forget that there are primary differences in how we relate to each other. Remember, in most cases both parties are trying to communicate in good faith, and it helps to consider gender differences before assuming anything different.

Men Are Thinkers, Women Are Feelers (generally speaking, of course)

Why do there seem to be clear and fundamental differences between men and women? Why do men tend to want to talk about external issues and women tend to want to talk about internal ones? This has much to do with how they make decisions and determine what is important.

For example, the Myers-Briggs Type Indicator, perhaps the most widely used tool for measuring individual styles and preferences, distinguishes between how "thinkers" and "feelers" make decisions and communicate them to others. Thinkers believe that the best decisions are rational, logical, and dispassionate and that everything is governed by objective, consistent rules. There are absolute rights and wrongs, and the rules can't be changed to fit a situation. They think that emotions can distort and negatively affect the quality of decisions.

Feelers, on the other hand, highly value emotion when making and acting on decisions. Their frame of reference is subjective. Making a sound decision means that everyone involved should feel as good as possible. To feelers, there are no absolute rights and wrongs. The most effective way to behave is to accommodate all styles. Their approach is sensitive to emotion and unconcerned about whether everything makes perfect sense.

Not surprising, two-thirds of all men who take the Myers-Briggs score highly as thinkers, and two-thirds of all women score highly as feelers. Again, these are general ideas; the important thing is to remember that everyone, regardless of gender, is unique. This means that we must relate to people first and foremost as individuals.

Communication Tips for Men and Women

If we understand ourselves and the opposite sex better, and make some slight adjustments, we'll be able to bridge the communication gap between us.

> *"You don't have to see the whole staircase, just take the first step."*
> —**Martin Luther King Jr.**

Listening and Body Language

The first thing that is different between us is the way we listen. Men and women do listen to each other, yet they do it differently. Women, generally speaking, listen actively and often nod and smile. Men rarely do this. Men think of the nodding and smiling as agreement, seeing it as a sign encouraging them to speak. One woman I know was turned down for some business because of her continual nodding—the client thought she agreed with everything and made no decision on her own! He thought she was weak, she thought she was being polite! The client exhibited common male listening traits: wandering gaze and neutral facial expression. Many women think this is rude and inattentive. As a result, women may act defensively when men don't even realize that their listening can trigger this behavior!

A tip to women when we are networking with men: Cut down on the nodding and smiling and lessen the intensity of your gaze.

A tip to men: Keep steadier eye contact and assume nothing if you see a smile or nod.

Changing Topics

Men often feel that interrupting someone is the logical way of changing speakers, while women often wait for their turn out of politeness. Women need to jump in or they may wait a long time to speak at an event or meeting!

Advice to women: Learn to jump in—this is a skill. Speak a bit louder, faster, and with more enthusiasm. Give a comment about what is being said, such as, "John, you're right, that seems relevant, and here is another point to consider." Keep the rapport going without pausing, and know that you'll be interrupted.

Advice to men: Interrupt less and wait for pauses in the conversation. Ask a woman what she thinks and then you'll get feedback.

On the Lighter Side

Humor and jokes:

Women: Know that men exchange a lot of one-liners and learn to follow. Just know that if the ball is tossed your way, you can throw it back. Keep it positive.

Men: Know that women prefer indirect communication, such as, "Good morning. How was your weekend?" instead of: "You look exhausted. Didn't you sleep last night?"

Making Small Talk

For small talk, find gender-neutral topics, such as trends in the industry and current events rather than too much family conversation. Also, women tend to talk about themselves and their feelings more than men do. Men need to realize that this is just a woman's way of making small talk at times.

TIPS FOR MEN AND WOMEN TO "MEET IN THE MIDDLE" WITH COMMUNICATION SKILLS

Communication Skill	How Women Can Improve	How Men Can Improve
Listening	Cultivate a blank face	Maintain eye contact and listen without interrupting
Speaking	Jump in, increase volume, begin on a positive note	Wait for pauses in the conversation and avoid jumping in
Small Talk	Minimize talk about yourself	Talk about something other than sports
Humor	Go with the flow and learn to respond to joking politely	Avoid trying to be too witty and telling jokes that not everyone will appreciate

Tying It All Together

Building the right communication skills is a key to effective networking. These can be as simple as making eye contact and remembering people's names. Understanding the variety of personality types out there, coupled with the knowledge of men's and women's basic "wiring" when it comes to communication styles, can greatly enhance your networking opportunities. It will be a more satisfying experience for you and those with whom you network. Now that you have the basics of understanding others and making contact, we will look at personal marketing—how to best present yourself in the "grocery store of life."

Exercise 1: How Do You Communicate?

The following list contains eight essential communication skills for effective networking and life skills. Rate yourself on a scale of 1 to 5, where 5 is the highest and 1 needs improvement. Mark the skill(s) on which you didn't rate highly (1–3). What's holding you back? What can you do to improve these skills?

- Smiling
- Looking the person in the eye
- Listening
- Remembering names
- Being aware of body language
- Respecting other people's boundaries
- Looking for common interests
- Giving genuine compliments

Exercise 2: Complimenting Others

Make a list of five co-workers or people with whom you associate and write down at least two compliments you can give each person. Pick a day when you will see them all, and use the Five-a-Day penny exercise described in this chapter. Your goal is to transfer all five pennies!

Name _____

1. _____

2. _____

Name _____

1. _____

2. _____

Name _____

1. _____

2. _____

Name _____

1. _____

2. _____

Name _____

1. _____

2. _____

Exercise 3: Are You Listening?

I often say that listening is the most effective skill in being a successful business networker. Now it's time for you to see if you can retain what other people tell you.

Talk with other people at your office or at a meeting about any of the topics we've covered so far. After you speak with them, summarize three things that stood out from what was discussed and answer the following questions:

What were you able to remember from what they said?

_____

_____

_____

What do they remember about you?

_____

_____

_____

Is that what you wanted them to remember?

_____

_____

_____

How can you improve your communication so that people remember what you want them to?

_____

_____

_____

_____

Exercise 4: Characteristics or Best Practices of Great Networkers

Who Is Good?

Write down the names of at least two people you consider to be good networkers, then write down what characteristics they have that you think help them succeed.

1. _____

_____

_____

2. _____

_____

_____

Are You Effective?

Look at the traits of effective networkers. Rate yourself on a 1–5 scale, where 5 is the highest and 1 is the lowest. Mark which ones you need to improve on (1–3). What strategies can help you make those areas stronger?

____ Friendly and approachable

_____

____ Confident

_____

____ Empathetic

_____

____ Appreciative of others' help

_____

____ Tenacious in overcoming obstacles

_____

____ Enthusiastic and energetic

_____

____ Caring

_____

____ Good listener

_____

____ Rebound quickly from rejection

_____

____ Nurture relationships

_____

____ Appearance

_____

"A journey of a thousand miles begins with a single step."
—Chinese proverb

CHAPTER 5

Your Best Foot Forward

recently connected two friends. Randy is in the insurance business, and Joel is a CPA. I thought there might be some synergy between the two and they had a good first meeting—"good" meaning that they sincerely enjoyed meeting each other, yet what business connection might be made was not apparent.

Then we all happened to be at a business cocktail party, and as we were casually talking, Randy mentioned his supervisor. Joel's eyes lit up and he said, "You work with Bill? That's great to hear! He's terrific and someone I respect a lot. Can we talk again next week and set up a time when the three of us could meet? I've read what Bill has said about developments in your company and I'd like to share some helpful ideas that might fit into your plans."

Later, as Randy and I were talking, he said, "Isn't that amazing what happened as soon as I mentioned Bill?" I said, "Yes, and it is truly remarkable when people get connected and then find something in common and the conversation seems to flow better as your interest in each other increases." In this case, it was a true win/win situation and the connection was made.

A phrase I love sharing is: the opposite of networking is not working. When used positively and correctly, networking can be the most important business skill you can use anywhere you go. Every time you meet someone, you have an opportunity to learn from that person and to be a resource as well. Remember, you can even learn from someone you don't like or respect in that you can learn what not to do or how not to act. Often in my workshops I say that and everyone agrees. We see in other people what we either want to emulate or avoid doing.

Networking is at its best when our interpersonal skills create an atmosphere of respect and trust. We all want to do business with people who make us feel comfortable. This chapter focuses on what it takes to present yourself as someone with character and integrity. Read the newspapers to learn about how business leaders conduct themselves. CEOs with integrity are respected (those without it go to jail). It is about putting your best foot forward and selling yourself.

CHARACTER CHECKUP

When you want to evaluate the character of someone with whom you would like to network, here are some questions to consider:

- Does the person look you in the eye when speaking or do his or her eyes roam around the room?

- When you help someone out with a referral or contact, does the person acknowledge what you did?

- Does the person answer questions honestly?

- Do you get a sense that the person is sincere or simply sees you as a business target?

Nobody is perfect; however, character does matter. Make sure the people you connect with have integrity and be sure to watch your conduct as well.

"The only place where success comes before work is in the dictionary." —**Vidal Sassoon**

Self-Marketing

Many years ago when I was selling advertising space for a trade division of Macmillan, I got a call mid-morning from one of the senior vice presidents who asked if I was free for lunch with him and the president of the division. Of course, I went. However, when I look back on all the mistakes I made, I shudder. For some crazy reason that particular day, I was going to be in the office all day, so I wasn't dressed in my normal business meeting style. If that weren't enough, I was also too immature at the time to use the sage advice I have since learned, "Talk less and listen more." I came across as a flighty kid instead of as someone who could have been groomed for a new job opportunity. Granted, I had the business credentials, but I didn't do a good job of marketing myself.

Fast forward many years later. I'm still friendly with that vice president, who has since retired after serving as chairman of a major corporation. It's great to remember how I have learned over the years that you *always* have to be ready to present your "self-brand."

Think of some well-known brands that you use. Why do you always go back to them? What makes them stand out in your mind? Usually the reason you remember them is twofold: marketing and consistent quality.

We are surrounded with marketing for new ideas and products. In this book, the focus is on the opportunity to market the most important product each one of us has, ourselves.

The way we appear, communicate, interact, and are perceived by those in our workplace and by our clients is a direct result of the tools we develop as self-marketers. The Carnegie Institute of Technology did some research, which was confirmed by other studies, showing that technical skills account for 15 percent of financial and career success, while interpersonal skills account for 85 percent. I believe much of our success comes from our efforts to build a network of people who fully appreciate our talents, recognize our potential, and support us in getting where we want to go. Remember, it's a two-way street. You should always be looking for those people whom you can help.

Your Personal Brand

So, what is you own personal "brand?" It is how you express who you are and what you have to offer. Think of the vision you wish to create. The brand you develop for yourself is what people will think of when they hear or see you. As for me, I've been branded as the "Queen of Networking." (This title stuck because that's one way the *Wall Street Journal* has referred to me.) It opens doors and opportunities all the time, and it came about because I am a stickler for consistency, reliability, and staying connected, all essential networking skills.

Your brand will create buzz, and that informs more people about you.

YOU ARE THE PRODUCT

Answer these questions as you "package" your brand:

- Why did you choose to go into the business you're in?
- What types of people do you most enjoy serving?
- How do you uniquely help those people solve their problems?
- With whom do you compete, and what do they do well that you should work to do as well?
- What makes you different from the competition that your current clients like?

A brand is simply what people think when they hear a name or see a logo.

THE GROCERY STORE OF LIFE

If you were sitting on the shelf, like a box of cereal, why would someone decide to buy you?

- Do you grab people's attention?
- What "ingredients" do you list that are better for the consumer?
- Are you new and improved?

Cap'n Crunch cereal has been around for many years, yet today's version is healthier and has an updated image for today's consumers. (It's okay for you to be sweet, just not sugary.)

THE SELF-MARKETING ALLIANCE THREE-POINT SYSTEM

Look at how world leaders build alliances between their countries. It takes planning and patience. Look at the European Union. Years ago it was just a dream; today it's a powerful collaboration. Here's how you can do the same:

1. **Be known.** Go out and speak and write. Be a presence in your community. Be sure to keep a high profile among the people you are aligned with.

2. **Be liked.** Take good care of people, and they'll take care of you. Your allies will want to hear from others about how much you respect people.

3. **Be trusted.** Be a true professional always and true to your word. Your reputation will precede you, especially when others are saying good or bad things about you. Your allies want to know from others that their association with you is an asset.

When you've created a recognized brand for yourself, your clients, friends, and contacts will be your biggest advocates, and they will refer prospects to you. You have credibility in their eyes.

Think of what distinguishes you from others in the same business. Think about what you are best known for and write it down. Why are you known for that? Back it up with some examples.

Create Alliances

When you read newspapers, you often see how stories about political and social causes, including such words as "coalition," "pact," and "associations." These are people and organizations that join together for a common good. There is strength and many benefits in joining forces. The same is true when building your network of people.

I met Gail, who has her own consulting business, more than three years ago at an industry networking event. After the event, I followed up with a suggestion to meet for lunch, and we have kept in touch ever since. I stay on her radar through my newsletters. Later, we decided to create an alliance where we could sell one another's services. Recently, she called to tell me that several of her clients were interested in my services. She had made calls and sent notes to people, and some opportunities were starting to develop. I am doing the same for her. I believe that the essence of self-marketing is convincing others to believe in you and to become your advocate. This is very different from self-promotion, which often comes across as aggressive and negative.

I spoke with Gail recently to thank her for all the connections she has started to make for me. Her answer has stuck with me: " You make me look good in front of my clients." Again, all the more reason to develop your alliances and connections through trust and respect. Ask yourself as Gail did about me, "Would I want that person representing me or to be a reflection on my hard-earned and developed contacts?"

Become a Resource for Others

We all have skills and knowledge that can be helpful to others. When you become a resource for others, people will recognize your expertise, refer you, and help your network grow.

One day I received a call from Jim, who was referred to me as someone who might help him find a job. I was happy to help him, and in turn, he offered many resources that helped me. Through our several phone meetings, I met more than ten people and received two new projects, and Jim got his dream job through one of the connections I made for him. Both of us work our networks and believe first in giving and helping others. The result benefits both of us.

Making yourself an "expert" in an area is important. People remember what you are best known for and what expertise you have. Just think of some of the various products and services you use and why. Which product comes to mind when you think of a dependable family car? Fast pizza delivery? Delicious dinner for two? High-speed Internet connection? Just as is the case with these products, your goal needs to be that your contacts see you as "the only person" who can help them in certain areas.

What skills, expertise, and resources do you have that you can give to others? How can you best communicate this? Here's a way to begin.

1. **List your skills that you think can help others.** Persuasive writing skills, excellent computer knowledge, go-to person for finding suppliers. I think of my computer consultant, John. He's a whiz on the computer, which makes my life easier, and he speaks in human terms, not in digital computer language.

2. **List areas in which you are knowledgeable.** This includes specific comprehension of your industry or any new developments and trends in your field. Allan is a dentist extraordinaire. He is continually reading, taking courses, and learning new advances in the protection and care of teeth and is always full of advice and tips on how to best care for my teeth.

3. **Think of people, places, and things you know about that would be helpful to others.** Office equipment, Web sites, restaurants, stores, workshops and seminars, newsletters and recent articles, trade organizations, and the like—I continually learn new information and trends from everyone and every source in my network, and I share it with the people in my alliance to show that I am a team player.

My friend, Bruce, is a master at being a resource to others. He researches twenty to thirty magazines and papers every week and sends out e-mail memos to his database according to their interests. I am on several of his lists and always find the information interesting and helpful. What is Bruce doing besides giving out great information that he has researched? He is staying on many people's radar screens, and the "buzz" about him continues.

His mastery of networking goes even further. Bruce will also send a letter to two different people making an e-mail introduction and letting each person know something about the other and why they would want to connect.

4. **Help others fine-tune their thirty-second infomercials.** We all need a good sounding board to test how well we communicate our image. Ask the people in your alliance to tell you what they do in a clear, concise, compelling statement. Then critique their "infomercials" and offer suggestions to make them better. A friend once told me in astonishment about how she overheard someone say that people were describing her to others as a "specialist in landscape photography." Actually, my friend had just started a studio for children's portraits, yet in conversation she had mentioned something about her landscape photos, not her new children's studio. While she was flattered to be mentioned to others, she realized she had not communicated her current focus on children's portraits.

As it turns out, my photographer friend was not only speaking with someone who had children of her own (potential client), but who was also on the board of directors of a riding school that taught children with handicaps. Another photographer found this out, volunteered to take publicity photos for the school, and ended up with several paying clients.

5. **Supply people in your alliance with support materials.** Make sure that members of your alliance have copies of your newsletters, business cards, and articles you've written. Of course, get the same materials from them to distribute as well.

6. Share speaking opportunities. If you are invited to speak on a panel, find out if the presenting organization needs more presenters. If so, contact appropriate people in your alliance to join you. This can even work for writing articles or creating a noncommercial, information-based Web site where you and several of the people in your alliance make information available.

The most important attitude with those in your close circle is to be a giver and to share every resource that helps to develop the partnership and builds greater trust.

Personal Power

Communicating a sense of inner strength comes from a belief that you are determined to reach your goals. Powerful people empower others and encourage them to express themselves openly. You communicate a sense of personal power by developing these traits:

Authority: Authority is inner confidence, a trust in your skills and abilities. It comes from an attitude of "I can do that." This attitude radiates outward as you politely assert your knowledge to establish who you are while, at the same time, helping others.

Assertiveness: Assertive behavior is active, direct, and honest. By being firm, we view our wants, needs, and rights are equal with those of others. An assertive person wins by influencing, listening, and negotiating so that other people choose to cooperate willingly. There is a thin line between being assertive and being aggressive. When it comes across as attacking and arrogant, it's aggressive. When you are firm and getting your point across, it's assertive.

Accessibility: The powerful person is a master networker. Good networking increases your visibility and provides you with a valuable circle of people to whom you can give and from whom you can receive support and information. Imagine yourself as the hub of a wheel surrounded by spokes (your contacts).

Image: You communicate power through your image. Do you project an image consistent with strong leadership? Stand tall and walk proudly, but with humility. Always remember that you have value as a person regardless of anything negative people may say about you. When you meet others, make direct eye contact and keep your handshake firm and friendly. Clearly state who you are and what you do.

Confidence is a key ingredient in projecting personal power. Often I ask my classes, "Who here, besides me, would like to buy some confidence?" Almost every hand goes up. Unfortunately, confidence is not something you can buy. You have to work at it. Confidence comes from experience, making mistakes, doing something over and over again until you get it right, and being proactive.

Think how much more confident you are today in your job than you were the first week, month, or year. How much more comfortable are you speaking in public than you were when you first took the podium? Building confidence takes time and patience.

First Impressions Count—Appearance

It takes only three seconds to make an impression. While we all believe we should be judged on our character and innate worth, unless that first impression is a positive one, we often do not get the chance to reveal who we truly are. That's why it's worth the time to look our best whenever we come in contact with those we need in our network, which is all the time, everywhere. This doesn't mean you have to wear the latest trends and fashions. My style is to dress on the conservative side, always looking professional and "when in doubt, leave it out!" (e.g., pins for religious or political organizations). If you simply follow a few commonsense guidelines for looking your best, you can turn that first impression into a gateway to making profitable connections.

A colleague, Sarah, told me an unfortunate story that may have happened to someone you know. Sarah left New York late on a Sunday afternoon to fly to Los Angeles to present a training program the next morning. She decided to fly in comfort in jeans and sneakers, with no carry-on except her handbag and a book. She checked her bag at the curbside check-in.

At nine o'clock that night, when her bag didn't come off the plane in Los Angeles, panic set in. How could she show up to teach a class on communications at nine the next morning in jeans and sneakers? Lucky for her, an all-night discount store was open, and somehow she was able to piece together a navy suit, panty hose, and a pair of shoes. Believe me, these were not high-quality fashion items. It was a miracle that she was able to look presentable when she greeted her class the next morning. However, she did confide to me that her improvised wardrobe affected her confidence.

After I heard her story, I told her my two travel rules: First, always dress professionally when traveling. You never know whom you may meet and, if something happens to your luggage, you have an outfit; second, always carry on a bag with enough essentials to make it through a day.

Networking Etiquette

"Hello, my name is Linda," she said, walking over and introducing herself to Sharon, whom she met in line at an event. Without knowing how the other would react to a complete stranger, both began an eclectic discussion, ranging from Linda's childhood career dreams to Sharon's current endeavor as a personal shopper for clients interested in shopping in Paris.

After about twenty minutes, someone rudely interrupted them by standing right in front of Linda and completely taking over the conversation. The man introduced himself to Sharon as the publisher of a magazine, but failed to acknowledge Linda. Taken aback, Linda only stayed there in an attempt to join the conversation he began about advertising. He never even looked at her. When the time was right (Linda's goal was to maintain her composure and redirect any negative feelings away from the situation), she injected herself back into the conversation by explaining *her* position as a media buyer. To the man's total surprise, she turned out to be a buyer for one of his top accounts.

He started to realize that perhaps he was selling the wrong person and decided that Linda was now worth speaking to. She was turned off, however, and never gave him her card or expressed any interest in talking further. She did get Sharon's card, though, and the two have stayed in touch and laughed at the circumstances under which they met.

It was truly poor networking etiquette or negative networking, as I call it. Networking is all about establishing relationships and building trust instead of trying to make a quick sale.

TUNING INTO THE RADIO IN YOUR HEAD

There are two radio stations constantly playing in our heads. Which one you tune into more often determines how successful you are at networking. Take a listen:

WII-FM—which stands for **W**hat's **I**n **I**t **F**or **M**e. Unfortunately, this one often spells trouble because it tells the other person that you are only interested in getting something and usually now.

MMFI-AM—**M**ake **M**e (the other person) **F**eel **I**mportant **A**bout **M**e. I work at always tuning into this station. I ask myself, "What can I do to make the other person feel good and build rapport?"

A survey we conducted asked our participants: "What is the worst thing someone did to you when "networking?" Here's what we learned:

Option	Response
Seemed interested only in selling me something	44%
Left as soon as he/she realized I wasn't someone who could help them	26 %
Talked only about himself/herself	14%
Gave advice I didn't ask for	9%
Asked too many personal questions	7%

As you can see from the survey, when you only tune into yourself, others want to turn you off!

Once at a seminar, George, a quiet man, raised his hand to share his worst experience. At a cocktail party, he talked with one woman, and later in the evening, she came back to him and said, "Please give me back my card. I realize that you can't help me." I know your jaws may have just dropped because, while it's true, it's difficult to believe. You would be surprised at some of the negative networking that goes on.

Etiquette is good manners and common courtesy. Growing up, most of us learned our manners from our parents, school, peers, and mentors. A friend told me about a young investment banker who attended a dinner with his boss and a potential client at a swanky restaurant. Uncertain of the proper dining etiquette, he learned to survive by closely observing the manners of others. While it worked in this situation, he knew that to really survive in the corporate world, he would have to learn the rules of business etiquette.

To the right are some etiquette tips and techniques to help you out in many networking and business situations.

Check Your Business Etiquette Skills

Q. At a business meal, when should I start the business discussion?

Your answer:_____

_____

Andrea's suggestion: It's a good idea to let your guest have an appetizer and a drink before starting to discuss business. At breakfast, let the other person have some coffee and a bite of muffin. Use that time to get to know the person through casual conversation.

Q. After an initial meeting, what is the best way to follow up?

Your answer:_____

_____

Andrea's suggestion: It is best to send a handwritten note instead of an e-mail, which most people use to communicate. E-mail is immediate, but a handwritten note shows that you took the time. I often send a quick e-mail first, but I always follow that with a handwritten note, which is my "trademark."

Q. I'm expecting an important call. Do I leave my cell phone on during a networking meeting?

Your answer: ❏ Yes   ❏ No

Andrea's suggestion: Never leave the ringer on; turn it off and put the phone on vibrate only. Then, when you feel it go off, you can excuse yourself at the right time and check for messages in private. This rule also applies to any other personal electronics that could start buzzing or ringing at a bad time.

Q. I'm going to a networking event and have been advised to hand out at least twenty-five business cards. Is this a good goal?

Your answer: ❏ Yes ❏ No

Andrea's suggestion: No. A better goal is to make a certain number of quality contacts and to follow up after the meeting. Just handing out your card is not making a quality connection. I once watched a man enter a networking event, walk around, and hand his card to the first twenty people he met. He just said, "Hi, I'm [name] with [his company name]. Here's my card. We can help you save money on [his product]." I'll bet he told everyone the next day how many "contacts" he made, and how hard he "networked." I don't think so.

Q. I'm looking for new clients. Should I send a mass e-mail to my contact list asking for referrals?

Your answer:_____

_____

Andrea's suggestion: No. Thoughtfully go through your list and send a personalized message or call each person you feel may be of some help or might give you advice on finding new business.

Q. I'm trying to get business from a company. I know that a friend of a contact of mine knows the director of marketing. Should I use that person's name when calling for an appointment?

Your answer:_____

_____

Andrea's suggestion: Do this only when you have permission from both parties, your contact and his friend. Also, take the time to learn something about each of them. Be sure to send a thank-you note to each and let them know what happened.

Common Networking Situations and Rules of Etiquette

I was at an event and I noticed Jill, an association manager, rushing into the program, which was already in progress. The registration desk was closed so she had no name tag, was frazzled, had missed the short networking time before the seminar began, and had a hard time calming down to listen to the program. During the lunch break, she started talking to a woman in the line for drinks. When Jill wanted to give her a business card, she couldn't find them! She had changed purses at the last minute and forgotten to transfer her card case.

Jill was so anxious that she spent the ten-minute break searching for a stray card instead of listening to her new colleague, who eventually moved on to someone who would listen to what she was saying.

Jill hurried to another group, pushing in aggressively in her haste not to waste any more time. She blurted out her name and thrust her hand at one person in the group. Everyone politely backed away from her as they hurried to their lunch tables. During the meal, Jill just couldn't relax. She spoke too much, talked with her mouth full of food, and managed to offend everyone around her.

Ironically, I know Jill, and she's a nice person. What I also know is that she doesn't do well under pressure or when everything doesn't go according to plan. What can we learn from Jill?

Following are some common networking situations and rules of etiquette that address the negative approach that Jill took.

At a Networking Event or Meeting

1. It's better to arrive early than late. Arriving late signals that you think your time is more valuable than the time of those at the meeting. An early arrival shows enthusiasm for the event and respect for other people's time. An added benefit is that an early arrival gives you the opportunity to meet more people.

2. Place your name tag on your right-hand lapel. This places it in direct eye contact with the person you meet and allows others to see who you are and to remember your name when they are shaking your hand (assuming you're right-handed).

3. Exchange business cards with ease. Place your cards in your right-hand jacket pocket where you can easily access them. Make sure you have enough to last through the event. Be sure they are fresh and don't look like they've been collecting lint in your pocket. Place the cards you receive from the people you meet in your left-hand pocket. This way you won't inadvertently give out someone else's card thinking it's your own. Or remember your networking tool kit and have two attractive business card cases, one for your cards and one for those you receive.

4. Make eye contact and keep it. Looking someone in the eye shows respect and interest. People can always tell when your eyes are wandering over the room looking for your next contact. What you are silently saying is, "You are not that important to me." This isn't the message you want to communicate.

5. Shake hands firmly. There is nothing worse than a fish-like or death grip handshake. Make your handshake firm and professional.

6. Be aware of personal space. Moving in too close makes people uncomfortable. Most people consider anything closer than eighteen inches to be too close and will back away from you.

7. Join conversations in progress with grace. Be sure to ask for "permission" to join a conversation. Say something like, "This looks like a fun group, may I listen in?" People enjoy having you join them when you are courteous.

8. Exit a conversation politely. Express pleasure at having met the individual and the hope that you will meet again.

9. On eating and carrying on a conversation: simple. Don't do it.

10. On drinking and carrying on a conversation: a nonalcoholic drink without ice is the easiest to handle. Why no ice? Frigid handshakes are not pleasant. Why nonalcoholic? You'll pay better attention.

Meals—At Large Events or Private Functions

People were walking into the meeting room at the hotel to an industry cocktail party and dinner. Jim was very visible and audible in that he was trying to manage his beeping digital organizer and his ringing phone while balancing a drink and a plate. As he walked around talking to people, he kept peering into his Blackberry and kept his cell phone in his hand, just in case it rang. By the time everyone sat down for the meal, Jim was hungry, so he started eating before it was appropriate. He tried to talk over everyone and started a conversation with one of the guests at the far end of his table, which made for an uncomfortable situation.

Unfortunately, he also picked up his neighbor's glass of water and used the wrong fork for the salad. Poor Jim—on top of all of this, he jumped right into a sales pitch at dinner, letting everyone at the table know who he was and what his company does.

Sad for Jim. His picture should be in the dictionary next to "negative networking." Look below to see how he might have done much better.

1. Turn off your cell phone and handheld e-mail device. Talking or, worse, making a call during a meal shows disrespect. It says, "The person I'm talking to is more important to me than you are." One woman I know thinks she is being sly by having her handheld e-mail device in her hand and casually peering into it. Everyone knows what she's doing and it's rude.

2. Introduce yourself first to the person seated to your right and your left. Then introduce yourself to the rest of the table. As others join your table, introduce yourself and others to them. You may even arrange with another colleague at the table to switch seats with you during a second course or dessert so that you both get to know more people.

3. Wait for the head table to begin eating or, if it's a private meal, wait for the host or hostess to begin. When you are the host or hostess, you must begin first.

4. When ordering, allow your guest(s) to order first. Direct the server first to your guest(s), then select your entrée. It is safest to pick something in the mid-price range and something easy to eat. Remember, it's not about the food, it's about making connections.

5. Chose your fork wisely. If you're unsure about which utensil to use, working from the outside in is the safest bet. Alternatively, watch the host, hostess, or other guests and do as they do.

6. Keep your napkin in your lap until you leave the event or restaurant. If you leave the table temporarily, leave the napkin on your chair.

7. Not sure which water glass or salad plate is yours? Remember, liquids on the right, solids on the left. If your neighbor forgets and takes yours, just ignore it.

8. When you're finished, place your knife and fork in a parallel position across the center of your plate, handles on the right. This signals the waiter to clear your setting.

9. Even if you are still hungry, stop eating when everyone else is done. Slow eaters beware. You can always get a snack later. Conversely, if you are a fast eater, slow your pace to match others.

10. Never talk with your mouth full. Yes, I know, you learned this when you were six. At your next event, just watch how many adults still do this and make sure you're not one of them.

11. Refrain from talking about business until after people have settled in and had their appetizers. This allows ample time for small talk and getting acquainted.

REMEMBER, YOU'RE ALWAYS "ON"

Recently I was invited to make a sales presentation to a company, and when I met the executive vice president, I thought she looked vaguely familiar although I couldn't place her. During my presentation it hit me. The week before I had been at a restaurant having dinner with a friend and had noticed her at the next table because she was yelling at the waiter in a disgraceful fashion. Obviously I kept this revelation to myself. However, based on the scene at the restaurant, I decided that she might be a very tough client to work with. I declined the project. The incident reminded me that we should always be on our best behavior, because, in truth, we are always "on."

12. Ask before you take notes. It is perfectly acceptable to take notes at a business or networking meal, just ask first out of courtesy. Then use a small, attractive notepad and pen. Always keep these in your tool kit, ready to go.

Making Introductions

At an important meeting, Bill got nervous when he ran into Mr. Davis, the president of a large manufacturing company he wanted as his client. He was walking with an intern, Josh, who had started recently right out of college. As they approached, Bill said, "Mr. Davis I'd like you to meet Josh, who has just started with our company." Mr. Davis was professional and gracious, and he spoke for a few minutes with Bill and the intern, asked a couple of questions, and then made his exit. What did Bill do wrong? Here are a few clues:

1. In the business world, defer to position and age. Gender is not a factor. An introduction is normally made in a logical order:

   - Introduce younger to older.
   - Introduce your company peer to a peer in another company.
   - Introduce a junior to a senior executive.
   - Introduce a fellow executive to a client.
   - Introduce a personal contact to a business contact. For example, my friend Linda has accompanied me to an industry luncheon, and we find that we are seated with one of my clients. I would say to my client, "May I introduce my friend Linda? Linda, this is my client, Bob Smith."

2. When making introductions, give a brief statement about each person's interest or profession. In the best case, mention something the two might have in common. This is polite and gets the conversation going.

My client, John, is a master at this. As he introduces different people to me, he always tells me something about the other person and, in many cases, he mentions a common interest. We then have a perfect place to start our conversation and John can exit gracefully.

E-mail Etiquette

I'm one of those people who checks e-mail throughout the day and whenever I'm on the road or on holiday. It's just part of my DNA. One person told me, though, that after being on vacation she came back to seventeen hundred e-mails, many of them were spam. Even with a lot of our spam controllers, we still get too much of it; and these marketers are often very clever with their subject line so it almost seems like it could be a real message.

Today our business life does indeed revolve around e-mail. While e-mail is an essential business communication, it can be misunderstood if you do not follow certain conventions. E-mail lacks the vocal inflections of a phone call, the body language of face-to-face communication, and the impact of a handwritten note on fine stationery. Yet, we also do know that you can tell when an e-mail has some "attitude" and, one hopes, a positive attitude.

Here are some e-mail etiquette tips to make sure your messages are read and responded to promptly:

1. Keep your e-mails brief and focused. Think of how many you get and do the math on how long it takes to read each one. Brevity is the winner here. Consider the fact that the Lord's prayer is only fifty-six words, and the Gettysburg address is 226, and these are important documents!

2. Use meaningful subject lines. These are your "grabbers" and convince the recipient to open and read your message.

3. State your point as soon as possible and what action you want the other person to take. (Think of your e-mail message as a mini-presentation.)

4. When you need to send a long document, send it as an attachment. You might need to get permission first because spam blockers often deny e-mails with attachments.

5. Forward only important information, not jokes, chain letters, warnings about viruses, or other junk messages that circulate on the Internet. It is unprofessional, and if you get a reputation for sending them, all of your messages will get deleted.

6. Always re-read your message before you hit "send." Make sure your tone is what you want it to be. Avoid anything that could be construed as sarcasm or innuendo. Many a sad tale is told of how someone hit the button before re-reading what he or she just wrote in a moment of anger, passion, or stress.

7. Answer all e-mails within twenty-four hours. A quicker response is always better. Even if you don't have an answer, at least acknowledge that you received the message and will be in touch soon.

8. Let people know when you'll be away. When you know you won't be able to check your e-mail regularly, engage the automatic "away from my desk" message for your e-mails. Better yet, send out messages to key contacts that you will be leaving in a few days and ask if there is anything urgent they need before you go.

9. Find a way to monitor messages. Even when you travel for business, you can still check e-mail anywhere on your laptop or at a business center. If need be, have someone in your office check your e-mail and call you with anything urgent.

Phone Etiquette

Next to in-person meetings, phone calls are the second most important personal way to stay in contact. Here are some tips to make phone contact better.

1. Return all phone calls within twenty-four hours.

2. When making a call, ask if it is a good time to talk and follow the lead of the person you're calling.

3. State the purpose of your call and indicate how much time it might take to complete the conversation. If you think the call will take a half an hour, and the other person only has a few minutes, schedule another time to speak.

4. When leaving a message, state your name, purpose, and action needed clearly and succinctly. And, most important, when you leave your phone number, speak s-l-o-w-l-y and repeat it. I usually write my number in the air as I say it, which makes me slow down.

5. When calling a contact referral, state your name and who referred you. For example, "Hello, Andy. My name is Andrea Nierenberg. John Baker suggested I call you about customer service training. Is this a good time to talk for a few minutes?"

6. Never do other tasks while you're on the phone. People can hear you typing on your computer or shuffling papers. This shows you are not focused on them. Even if you're just reading your e-mail, you still can't concentrate on the person on the phone. One of my clients, Roger, told me a funny story. He was on the phone one day with a client and was reading his e-mails at the same time. He was reading one from his

wife and when he was ready to say goodbye to his client, he said, "Bye, Honey. I love you!" Remember, doing two things at once is doing neither one well.

Networking at Non-Networking Events

Some people think that nonstop networking means making new contacts at weddings, family gatherings, Boy Scout meetings, and even funerals. My response? It depends. According to the "Nierenberg dictionary," the purpose of a networking meeting is to share information and make business connections that could lead to referrals and business, and this happens over time through developing a rapport and trust. However, the purpose of a social gathering outside of work is usually to celebrate or pay respects. Does this mean that personal events are strictly off limits for establishing relationships that could relate to business? Absolutely not. Actually, there are distinct advantages to forming connections at personal events, the main one being that these are people whom you've known most of your life, or their friends and relatives are, so you have a common bond. You can share a built-in sense of trust and understanding that takes much longer to develop with total strangers. However, like everything else you've learned about proper networking, there are right and wrong ways to conduct yourself.

When I want to talk business at these personal events, I keep a few ideas in mind to prevent any embarrassment:

I. Ask permission to follow up at a more appropriate time. If I'm speaking to my cousin from St. Louis and I find out she's the head of human resource training, I ask for her contact information and inquire if it's okay to give her a call during business hours.

2. Remember where you are. At a funeral, for instance, you discover that the person next to you is part of a chamber of commerce networking group to which you'd like to be invited, wait until after the service, then ask him or her how best to follow up. Doing anything else would be considered very bad taste.

3. What do you do when someone else wants to talk business? If the other person is pushing to discuss business, graciously suggest, "Who would have thought we'd meet at this event? However, this is probably not the right place to discuss business, so may I give you a call tomorrow and we can discuss this further?"

4. Discreetly exchange business cards, if you must. First, ask permission before exchanging business cards. Then the exchange of cards should be as discreet as handing a tip to a maître d'. Another way of handling this situation is to inconspicuously write the person's name and number in your networking notebook (asking permission first, of course).

5. Play by the rules. Recognize that there are establishments, such as some private clubs, where conducting business simply is not allowed. Be sure to follow the prescribed behavior.

You Scratch My Back, and I'll Scratch Yours

For some, networking is all about keeping a score card. Something like, "Hey, I've given you three client leads, what about me? What are you going to do for me?" Personally, I believe it's always better to give than to receive and never to keep score! When you look at business leaders, from Andrew Carnegie to Bill Gates, you see how their generosity in giving to others gets them a lot of good press. The same can be true with you.

THE "GOLDEN RULES" OF EFFECTIVE NETWORKING

1. Respect other people's time; it's a precious commodity for everyone.

2. Offer to help others sincerely. People can tell the difference between an opportunist and someone doing a good deed for people.

3. Always show and convey appreciation. Gratitude can be in the form of a gift or a simple note of thanks. Either way, do it consistently.

4. Share information. If you know something that can help someone, pass it on. Imagine, if previous generations didn't leave us their knowledge, the world could not progress.

5. Follow up, follow through, and keep others in the loop: Avoid being a "missing in action" networker. Find a good reason to stay connected, even when there is no "breaking news."

When you give to others, you build up your own personal public image, which goes a long way in developing business contacts now and well into the future. Here is my advice on keeping track of exchanging favors when it comes to networking:

■ Give more than you get. Even when someone does a favor for you first, think about how you can return it and add something extra. If someone gives you a client lead, think about offering a referral *and* a small box of candy to say thanks for the referral.

■ Demanding a favor in return is a big mistake. Has anyone ever said to you, "You owe me big time." Lines like that make my skin crawl.

■ Have a "giving" attitude. Mother Teresa is much more famous than most people in the world. Was it her wealth? Was it her education? Was it her business plan? No. She was a giver who looked at life from an eternal perspective. Just be a giver, and it will come back to you in better ways than you ever imagined.

One of my favorite sayings is, "Give without remembering and receive without forgetting."

Networking: "Are We There Yet?"

Like children traveling in the back seat of a car, we can often get impatient and bratty at having to wait for hours to arrive at our destination. So often, when people network, they think, "Hey, I got the person's card, we've had lunch, I know what I can sell them, so why is it taking so long to get new business?"

Generating genuine trust with someone takes time and patience. The items at the top of your priority list might not even get an honorable mention on someone else's. Many of my best networking connections that led to new business took years. Yes, years, ranging from two to five.

Remember, your personal image has to last over the long term. Think about major brands of consumer products like Pepsi, Tide, and even Quaker Oats. They took years to develop into respected names in the minds of consumers. The same is true with you. When you plant your networking "seeds" with business cards or meetings, give them time to grow. Pull an apple off the tree too soon, and it's bitter.

Now you're ready to put your best foot forward and network successfully. We looked at establishing your personal "brand" through making alliances, becoming a resource, and showing respect for others. You know the basic rules of etiquette, from using your phone to making introductions. In the next chapter we tackle one of the most challenging aspects of networking: how introverts can network effectively. If you or someone you know is shy when it comes to meeting new people, get ready. You'll be surprised to discover that introverts have more going for them in networking than you would think.

Exercise 1: Did You Make the Connection?

After you have had a conversation with someone you want to connect with, ask yourself the following:

1. Were you able to remember what the person said? What topics did you talk about that could lead to further connections or networking opportunities?

2. What do you think the person remembers about you? How did the person respond to your thirty-second infomercial and the other information you wanted to communicate?

3. Were you able to establish a reason to make a further connection? How did it go?

4. Do you know how to get in touch with the person and if he or she prefers e-mail or phone—office, home, or cell phone?

Exercise 2: Self-Evaluation for Your Best Networking Traits

Take a look in the "networking mirror" to see what about you shines and what you should focus on when you network more frequently. Here's one exercise to help you:

1. Make a list of three things that you are comfortable doing in your business life. You might say, "I'm a good listener," "I enjoy setting up meetings," or "I always send people information to help them do their jobs better."

2. Now take those behaviors and look at the strengths you bring to your work and your networking opportunities. For example, "As a good listener, I am able to hear the most important information on a call and then direct the client to who and what can help him the most."

3. How do the things you wrote down distinguish you from others? You may find that you are more skillful than anyone else in your department in building relationships with people from other cultures.

"For lack of training, they lacked knowledge,
For lack of knowledge, they lacked confidence,
For lack of confidence, they lacked victory."
—Julius Caesar

CHAPTER 6

The Introvert's Networking Advantage: The Quiet Way to Success

"Obstacles don't have to stop you. If you run into a wall, don't turn around and give up. Figure out how to climb it, go through it, or work around it."

—Michael Jordan

A Quiet Networker's Success Story

When the door opened and I walked in to start a business development meeting with several executives at a company, Cyndi clearly struck me with her approach to communication. I had heard beforehand that she was a rising star in the corporation, yet her challenge lay in the fact that she was unable to look me, or her colleagues for that matter, in the eye. Her shoulders were slumped, she made no "small talk;" and, as she started to talk about some of her projects, she gave just the facts in a monotone voice. Then, like a lightning rod, she spoke about her newest project, which was an initiative she was starting. It was as if a different person emerged from the Cyndi we first met. Her voice changed, she came "alive," and she spoke in such a way as to paint a real word picture of what she was looking to accomplish.

What happened that transformed her from seemingly shy and withdrawn to a passionate communicator about her work? Bottom line, Cyndi is an introvert. As I got to know her, she explained some of the challenges she faced in the business world. She felt she had to be "on" continually to sell herself, which she didn't like at all. As we began to talk and work together, she saw that she could keep her own style and personality and still "market herself"—she could communicate her ideas and strengths in a positive way. As her perceptions changed, her actions did, too, along with the way her colleagues and management perceived her.

I've known Cyndi for seven years now, and she is currently a senior vice president of another large corporation, where she runs a whole business unit and frequently speaks around the country. When I visit with her, she always goes back to the time when we first met, when she never thought she would be able to "come out of her shell."

One way that I always spot the Cyndis or other quiet networkers when I do a workshop is by the response I get from my first question on my prework questionnaire: "When you hear the word, networking, what immediately comes to mind? How do you feel about networking for your career advancement?"

This ice breaker is very telling. People pour out their feelings, and what I usually hear is: "I hate it, I'm not good at it," or "I don't like having to sell myself" or "It's not me."

What people find out in the first few minutes of our session is that networking, as you already know from reading this book, is a state of mind. We continually network in the way we interact, connect, and build on our relationships, regardless of our style. It is truly the eye-opening part of the workshop and there's plenty of discussion about it, which starts us on the road to positive personal marketing. It helps many introverts continue to work in the most passionate and organized way, follow up with efficiency, and develop alliances with others in the organization who will market them.

The Introvert's Business Advantage

INTROVERTS

Recharge by being alone
Prefer to listen
Are thoughtful and reflective
Focus well
May be mistaken for aloof
Need time and space for self
Keep thoughts to self
React internally
Are quiet
Do not enjoy "small talk"
Listen first, speak later

EXTROVERTS

Energize by contact with others
Are talkative
Are action-oriented
Multitask well
Seem friendly and outgoing
Like to surround self with others
Can "think out loud" through talking
React externally
Are expressive
Love "small talk"
Speak first, listen later

Did you know that Albert Einstein, Dwight D. Eisenhower, and Colin Powell are all introverts? It sometimes surprises people to find out that there are some very famous introverts out there who have achieved great success and have left their mark on the world. The success they achieved came from being able to take what's inside and bring it to the outside, to share it with the world. Extroverts are naturally good at this. They are wired to live outside of themselves. Introverts, however, need more internal time. They also have to have a little understanding of themselves and some techniques to get what is inside to the outside.

Do you have any introverted friends, or are you yourself an introvert? Studies have shown that introverts account for 25 percent of the population while, you guessed it, extroverts comprise the other 75 percent. To be able to interact with the majority, introverts have to learn what their strengths are so they can be heard and fully appreciated. Here are some of the most important strengths introverts have in business.

Strategy and Organization Come Naturally

Let's say your company wants to be the number one provider of widgets in the country. First you make production plans, then create marketing and public relations plans, and finally send out a sales team. When many ideas have to be considered, assimilated, and organized, give this work to an introvert. Introverts like to put puzzles together and make them work in a synergistic way.

While an extrovert is often the first person out there shaking hands and making initial connections, the introvert busily works away at a "master plan" to systematically achieve his or her networking goals. It may be days later before an introvert actually starts making calls. Each approach has its benefits, and neither is wrong. Extroverts can generally build multiple relationships more quickly, which energizes them more and more. Introverts, on the other hand, intuitively know that they only have so much "people energy" available, so they will usually create a systematic plan to get the job done.

Problem Solving

Some introverts, because of their temperament, can be very intense problem solvers. This intensity is a definite advantage. For instance, introverts process through all the pros and cons of a situation, and they intuitively know where the snags will be. This can be a great asset when networking. While an extrovert may be able to offer a variety of possible solutions in a sales call, the introvert is often able to pinpoint the obvious solution on the spot, because of his or her ability to solve problems.

I recently benefited from the problem-solving skills of one of my introverted associates. I was telling three clients at lunch about my great fortune in possibly having a major TV network interview me for an international event. I said that it might be in front of the United Nations building, and while I was talking about it, two of the three people were right there with me, full of energy and enthusiasm.

Then Karen, the head of the department, whom I had noticed was sitting there pensively, quietly asked me, "Have you checked it out with the UN? Do you have all the details from them? Have you considered the insurance issues?" She continued her mental checklist of questions in a very organized manner.

I realized immediately that, no, I hadn't done or even thought about any of these things. I was too excited about the actual happening!

Thank goodness for her detailed, organized, quiet approach. At first I felt as if my bubble had burst and then I realized that she was right, and her approach and information were going to save me from a lot of headaches and panic. I learned not to get too excited and was saying a silent "thank goodness" that I work with a very organized and processed team whose members would have made sure that all details were taken care of beforehand.

Good Readers, Good Writers, Good Listeners

If I want to find out what's going on with one of my introverted business associates, I often ask the person if he or she is reading any good books. The answer usually is yes. Then a passionate discussion often follows. Books are the introvert's best friends. Many are very well read and have a broad understanding about a variety of topics. This is due to their natural need for more alone time, and that's exactly what it takes to get through a number of books a year.

If your company is going to a networking event and several large potential clients are going to be there, assign researching these companies to an introvert. The thrill of getting paid to go online to find the latest news on these prospects will almost be too much for the introvert to handle! Have the person put together a mini-summary of each of these potential clients for you and the other salespeople, and it will be a great resource for your entire team.

Introverts often feel much more at ease using the written word to communicate their ideas. If they're presented with the option of making a pitch in person or writing out a twenty-page proposal, the proposal almost always wins. For personal communication, e-mail is often introverts' best friend. Here they can lay out all of their ideas clearly and in the exact order they prefer. Writing also allows introverts to nuance their communication, using exact word choices to spell out their thoughts and feelings precisely. Extroverts can also effectively communicate through the written word, but introverts should use this to their advantage in networking. If they can use e-mail communication to get their networking process going, this will give them a great advantage once it comes to making the actual in-person connections.

Your introverted employees' ability to listen may be their greatest asset. Extroverts often find it amazing that introverts can sit and listen to another person for a long time. Extroverts' exuberance naturally makes them want to jump in and make a contribution. However, they often miss or do not share points because there isn't enough time for anyone else to communicate. For introverts, listening comes a little easier. In fact, they may just want to listen and go back, process the information, and then schedule another meeting to talk about solutions. Especially with sensitive clients, introverts can make a great impression with their listening ability. Introverts should know how rare a good listener is, and they should know the difference this makes to the customer. Customers often emotionally embrace their introverted vendors because they feel so cared for when others listen to them.

Dale Carnegie, the grand master of communications skills, always said in his classes that one of the top human relations principles is to let the other person do a great deal of talking—that is, listen to the person! This is music to introverts' ears, for they would rather listen than talk.

Think back to a time when you were at a meeting or event, and as you were introduced to someone, you asked some open-ended questions. What happened? Most likely, the other person started talking and sharing, and you most likely jumped in with other prompter questions. Before you knew it, you were getting ready to leave, and after your exit strategy, the other person probably commented to the host, or at least thought, "I enjoyed talking with you so much. What an interesting person!"

While you didn't say much, you did do the following:

- asked open-ended questions,
- paid attention to what the person said, and
- showed your interest with your eyes and ears.

This is the power of good communication and rapport-building skills. For any cynics reading this and thinking, "that seems manipulative," it is *only* if it's done insincerely. As I always say about anything we discuss in this book, it must be done with the utmost sincerity, credibility, and character.

Passionate Conversationalists

If introverts have a challenge, verbal communication might be it. They tend to process their ideas and feelings internally. Extroverts often *need* to verbalize ideas and feelings to get them sorted out. This can be a great advantage for the extrovert, especially in fast-paced environments where answers are needed *now*. However, introverts should be encouraged because there are a number of ways they can make sure their ideas are heard and considered. When introverts are passionate and knowledgeable about a given topic and have found a comfortable venue for sharing their views, they can be quite brilliant communicators and highly effective networkers.

Caring

It's hard to say that one temperament style is more caring than another. It's usually a matter of personal choice. The point is that even though introverts may hesitate to share as many of their feelings as their extroverted counterparts, they may care about a situation or business decision just as intensely. When an introvert says a few caring words, they have been chosen carefully, and each word has great emotional value attached to it. An introvert might use ten words to get his or her feelings across to someone, while an extrovert may use a hundred words to share the same emotion. They are both valid ways to show emotion and need to be appreciated for their different styles. If you are an introverted networker, you might want to go the extra mile and send a card or quick e-mail later to reinforce that you truly care about the situation.

Introverts Are Great Networkers

Introverts are quieter by nature, yet they are and can be great networkers. They just do it differently from the other 75 percent of the world. The important thing for introverts is to have a networking plan. This will provide structure to verbalize their feelings and ideas most effectively. Introverts, your ideas and input are needed; the idea is to work within your nature. This means being comfortable with the fact that you network differently and have your own style that may be different from the majority's. Also, you need to realize that personal marketing and networking is just as critical for introverts as it is for extroverts! The key is to grow in the areas you find challenging and to have a tool kit of skills that will help you get your valuable ideas out to the world around you!

Growing Your Introverted Networking Skills

I usually can spot the people who dread coming to my session on networking. How? From the survey I send out in advance. Here are some of the responses I get to the question, "What comes to mind when you hear the word, networking?":

"It's selling and I don't sell."

"I'm not good at it—I don't like asking people for things."

"It's sleazy."

"I don't have a gift of gab."

The list goes on and usually, just like Cyndi, whom I talked about at the beginning of this chapter, I can pick these people out as soon as I enter the room.

People in the session come to realize that all of us have our own best practices when it comes to networking and personal marketing, and however we connect these dots, positive alliances and advocates can help us with what we want to create.

Determine the Areas That Are Most Uncomfortable

What area of networking are you are most uncomfortable with? Is it starting conversations? Small talk? Giving presentations? Cold calling? Think about as many different networking opportunities as you can remember from the past. These can be in business settings, at social events, or at church. List the top three "I-strongly-dislike-doing" areas of networking. Post them on the wall. These are the areas that we're simply going to take some time to learn more about.

Develop a Learning Plan

Now that you have your top three "fear factor" topics of networking, it's time to start turning these into positives in your mind. I'm not saying that you'll ever love doing these things, but you can get to the point where you will no longer avoid them, and you'll have these skills in your net-working tool kit to use when the time is right.

Make a commitment to do some reading, go to a seminar, or get personal coaching in these areas. Work this into your yearly plan. I suggest giving yourself at least three months, and not more than twelve, to gradually get some training in these areas. Of course, this depends on how critically you need to get these skills in place. If you're developing a new sales territory and need to increase the business by 400 percent by next year, then an abbreviated period will have to do. The next step is to start to be purposeful in implementing this learning in your daily work life.

Set Goals for Personal Meetings, Business Parties, and Events

You've become familiar with the three areas of networking that you'd like to conquer. I hope the books, articles, seminars, and personal coaching have been helpful and encouraging. You've seen that this is something you can do with a little grit! Now the challenge is to set some attainable goals that will help you get started using these newfound networking techniques. What you want to do is to set goals for personal meetings, business parties, and events.

Often the hardest part is knowing how and where to start. For example, a client of mine, Doug, was overwhelmed. He knew he had to get out in the field and attend new functions and associations. Yet there were so many functions, he could literally go to something every day or three times a day, for that matter. I always say quality versus quantity, and it certainly applies here.

Doug made a list of the top priorities he wanted to get out of the associations he joined. He knew that unless he got involved and went to meetings, it would be a waste of time and money. He started by listing the top ten organizations from his local Chamber of Commerce and an industry organization to which his clients belonged.

He used the 2-2-2 strategy that I discussed in my first book, *Nonstop Networking*: he set a goal of going to at least two meetings of the group, meeting two people, exchanging cards, and arranging two follow-up meetings. Therefore, whether he joined the group or not, he had learned something and had expanded his network by two.

He then narrowed his list down to three organizations in which he knew he had a strong interest and whose mission he respected. He carefully cultivated people he knew would, like him, get involved in committees to become known in the organization. Over one year, Doug was able to incorporate these three organizations into his life with consistency, ease, and a positive impact.

Write down the associations in which you'd like to invest your time and money to help your career and continued business development.

What will be your time commitment each month?

What will you do to become known in the group? (Hint: serve on a committee, offer to speak, or write an article for the newsletter.)

With practice, these skills will start to become second nature. The key is not to give up. Again, we're not talking about changing your introverted nature. What we want to do is gently push ourselves out of our comfort zones, honoring who we are, while at the same time stretching beyond ourselves to reach out to others with all that is inside us.

Start in Your Comfort Zone and Work Your Way Out

Who are the people with whom you are most comfortable? Make a list of family members, friends, and business associates with whom you can establish a networking home base. These people are your comfort zone, so this is where you want to start using your newfound skills. These people will be the most forgiving when you take some risks and make mistakes. Remember, mistakes are natural. Be easy on yourself. Imagine learning to walk and soon you'll be running! They will also give you honest feedback. If the situation is appropriate, you may even tell them about your quest to build up these skills. They will be impressed that you are taking proactive steps to better yourself and still be yourself.

The challenge here is to get out of your comfort zone quickly. When you've had some success networking with those you are comfortable with, it's time to take some bigger risks. The best time to take a risk is when you've been successful. You're at the top of your game and your confidence is high. Is there a client whom you've been wanting to call, yet haven't been able to? Now is your time. Go for it! You might not strike gold on the first hit; the goal is to build habits that will make you successful in the long run.

Body Language

As we discussed in chapter 4, body language and our visual image are 55 percent of our communication. Introverts, be especially aware of posture. It's been said that, "Posture is the foundation of your presence." Make sure you look up and stand tall. If you're not in the habit of doing this, it might seem awkward at first. Soon it will become second nature, and you'll see that others find you much more approachable. Then they'll reflect the positive feeling you radiate back to you in their conversation.

Eye Contact

Introverted men, especially, should make eye contact. Women, both intro-verted and extroverted, tend to have less trouble with this. For most men, the tendency is not to relate face to face. Side to side is much more comfortable for some. Most of your interpersonal networking will be face to face. Make sure you stay focused on the person talking to you. This may not feel completely natural at first, so try to avoid "locking on" to the other person with your eyes. This is where it feels as if someone is trying to drill holes in your head. It is completely normal to look around a bit, yet your attention should always bounce back to the other person's eyes. And remember to look at the "third eye!"

Creating an Introvert-Friendly Networking Plan

Iintroverts' networking success can greatly increase with a plan. As we mentioned earlier, this will come easily for most introverts with their organizing and strategizing temperament. Everyone's plan is different. What I have attempted to do here is to give you some ideas that you can incorporate into your own personal plan. The important part of the plan is to maximize your strengths, but stretch yourself in areas that tend to not come as naturally. Consistency will be your best friend in following your plan. I suggest that you ask the following questions in making your networking plan:

What is my ultimate goal for networking? Is it finding new business? Developing current accounts? Becoming known in my industry or in one that I serve? What are my personal strengths as an introvert, and how can I maximize these in networking toward my goal? Are they organizational skills, writing skills, or problem-solving skills?

What is my strategy for blending my strengths for those areas in which I need to stretch? How much time will I spend networking through writing, e-mail, and the Internet? How much time will I spend networking on the phone? Do I have goals for myself in this? How much time will I spend networking in person? Again, what are my goals for these types of events? How can I stretch myself in this and also honor who I am as an introvert?

How can I integrate writing, phone work, and in-person networking into a system that will work for what I do? Will I use an opener letter before I call my contact? When appropriate, will I always try to get an in-person appointment when I am networking over the telephone? Can I use my organizational strengths to be more prepared for when I am in a person-to-person situation? How might I use my writing strengths to add to what I present in person?

What books and educational or coaching resources might I utilize to continue sharpening the areas in which I am strong, while not neglecting the areas that challenge me? Do I have a yearly schedule for this? Have I set some goals for reading articles or books that will help me improve this year?

Are there areas of personal development, such as making eye contact, having good posture, using proper etiquette, and/or developing character that I want to remind myself to use regularly?

Let's walk through some of the ways you can maximize your introverted temperament to develop new business.

Maximizing Your Writing Strengths

If you're in a fast-paced or highly interactive environment, you'll want to conserve your social energy to avoid being tapped out when you really need it. One technique that can work well for introverted networkers is maximizing the amount of written communication in their networking approach. A caution up front: the idea is to maximize this strength, not hide behind the computer screen because it's more comfortable than being face to face or on the phone with people. You'll still need to be personally out there as much as possible. Nothing substitutes for an in-person meeting.

Writing for Publications and the Web

Introverts can maximize their networking effectiveness and raising their profiles by writing articles for magazines, newsletters, newspapers, on Web sites, in newsletters, and in weblogs, or blogs (we'll talk more about that later).

What I often do when I'm looking through industry magazines is to see if they take contributed articles. If it looks like they do, I e-mail or call the editors to see if they are interested in an article. As they tell you about the topics they might be covering in upcoming issues, you might say that you'd like to send a one-paragraph proposal for an article you could write for them. Or, if you have an idea right there on the phone that is something you can really write about with proficiency, then pitch that and see what they have to say.

If they don't need an article at the time, let them know that you'd like to send them a letter with your information in case they ever need to interview someone in your field. I usually include a short, casual letter thanking them for their time and offering my time as a resource in case they need someone to talk about "XYZ" in their industry. I might also include an article I've written that might pertain or other articles for which I have been interviewed. If I think there's some potential with the publication, I put it in my follow-up plan (see chapter 8) and find ways to keep in contact periodically.

When you write the article, take your time and do a good job. Remember, this is the first impression people might have of you. If you have a good solid article, they will know it and appreciate the work you put into it, even if you never hear this from them. When I have an article published in a trade magazine, I often send it to my clients in the industry. This builds credibility and makes them feel better about working with me. I can also use the articles in the sales process. It is often easier to show than to tell someone that you're qualified for a project. Also remember trade show and convention magazines; they can be great places to get your name in print. Attendees often read through the magazine they got when they registered. Chances are they'll see your article, and you may get some leads.

It's often easier to get published on the Web than it is in print. Print is expensive and very valuable real estate in the written world. The Web is much more flexible, yet it can still be very effective. My articles often run first on a magazine or trade organization's Web site. Then later, after I have built credibility with them, they will "promote" my articles to their print edition. Usually the person in charge of the print magazine is different from the person in charge of Web site content. Make sure you contact the Web site editor directly. Building a relationship with that editor can often have a positive effect on your relationship with the print editor.

The print editor has come to trust your work because you've proven yourself on the site. And remember to thank both editors for all the connections you make. This is part of the "thank-you chain," discussed in the next chapter. It works well and is a consistent part of the plan.

Of course, if you have your own Web site, use these articles there as well. You may have to make them less industry-specific to reach a more general audience, but this is often easy to do. In fact, it is possible to use the same article and change it to fit a wide variety of industries. Remember, the material is fresh to the accountants, even if you already used it in the cosmetic industry. Just make sure you take the time to research each industry and customize your article it, using industry-specific buzzwords and phrases.

Another up-and-coming way to get your name out using the written word is the fascination today with "blogs." What is a blog? Blog, short for "weblog," is basically a diary or log of your thoughts about a particular topic that is posted on the Web for the whole world to see. Blogs are especially useful if you deal with cutting-edge news. For instance, if you're a political consultant, people can go to your blog and see if you have anything in there on the President's new initiative to reform Social Security. If you're an expert in your industry, or even if you're not, you can start a blog to get your thoughts out to see what people think. From there you can set up a message board for them to respond to your thoughts, or they can simply e-mail you if they would like to talk further. This can be a great way to make contacts on the Web. If your blog is particularly good, people will start to add it on the "links" page of their Web sites. Soon you can become the "expert" in your particular area of interest as the momentum of your blog grows on the Net.

Online Networking Communities

There is a growing phenomenon on the Internet called the "online networking community." These communities undoubtedly have been created by introverts! Basically, for a fee, you can join a community and make contacts online. There are many ways to do this, the most common of which is to have each person set up a personal and business profile. Here you add as much or as little about yourself as you want people to know, then list the types of products or services you offer.

There's another place where you can post the things you're looking for. Are you looking for a new bookkeeper? Post it in the community, and people can respond to you. How about someone who would like to merge his or her small business with yours? Go ahead and post it. This can often open up a conversation online and then lead to face-to-face discussions. I am always an advocate of real live people getting together face to face. There is no greater form of communication. Try what's comfortable for you—it could be a way to meet people.

E-mail Networking

This can often be a good foot in the door. However, be careful not to "spam" people. People always read personal e-mails, yet are quick to recognize a form letter. Make sure each e-mail you send to a person is personally for him or her. There is nothing worse than sending your e-mail to the whole division of a company, and then, when you walk in the next week to meet with someone, they all realize you're the "spammer." (No, this has never happened to me—I've only heard the horror stories!) However, I do send out a monthly tip-of-the-month and a quarterly newsletter that often gets forwarded throughout a company. This is different from spamming. I also get a lot of responses to my tips and newsletters, and I answer each one personally.

The idea with e-mail is to get the conversation started, not close the deal. You might just follow up with someone you'd like to get to know because you saw the person mentioned in the newspaper or trade journal, heard about his or her recent success, or thought the person could benefit from a product or service you offer. You might not always get a response, but that's okay.

The next step is to get on the phone and talk with the person. Then at least you have an opener: "I'm following up on the e-mail I sent you about such and such." Usually the response is positive, such as, "Oh, I was meaning to get back to you." You may even put in your e-mail that you'll follow up via phone if that's appropriate. Again, the goal is to find common ground and eventually have a chance to talk with others face, particularly to face if you can really help them with a need, be a resource, or learn something from each other.

Opener Letters

Another technique to get things started is to use the opener letter. After I've determined whom I want to contact, I try to figure out how to customize a letter that might open some doors when I call the person to follow up. Usually, I try to work one type of business or industry at a time. For example, one month I concentrate on my prospects in the legal profession. During the following months, I may focus on real estate, cosmetics, fashion, and ad agencies, in that order. As I work on each industry, I do my best to follow its current trends by reading the paper and a few trade magazines every day, between appointments or while traveling. When I know I'll be writing my opener letter for a particular industry, I make sure to take written and mental notes as I do my reading.

Is there a current trend where I might be able to help people in an industry improve their communication skills in some way? Even new legislation that might affect a particular industry may provide a lead on where my services might be needed. The most effective way to write the opener letter is to know what's going on in the particular companies you are writing to. When I'm writing to an industry for the first time, I only research the top ten companies to which I want to reach out. This usually gives me a good idea of what might be happening in all of the companies I am contacting. The key is not to pretend you are the expert in your letter, just show them that you are informed and ready to let them know how you can be of genuine service to them.

There is no formula for writing an opener letter. The basic letter has an introduction, a body, and a conclusion or point of action you'd like the recipient to take. Introduce yourself, your product or service, and how you think you might be able to work together. In the body you might include some industry-specific details that grab the reader's attention, along with possible solutions that you could provide. In the closing, let the recipient know that you will follow up on the phone and give a specific time frame for when you will be doing this. Then make sure you follow up within that time.

By the way, you can also add a postscript to the letter. People often skip down to the P.S. to see what the letter is about without reading the whole thing. The idea is to capture your main idea and reiterate it in one or two sentences. For example: "P.S. Please remember, I'm offering a free consultation this month on how the art and science of networking can help you find, grow, and keep the best business relationships. Please call me at 888-555-1212, and we'll get together in person."

Using a Script

When you do get someone on the phone, ask if the person received your letter. If not, or if the person hasn't gotten to it yet, have a script ready to keep you from stumbling when this happens. Go through in your head all of the different answers you anticipate, from "Yes" to "I'm too busy right now" and have some idea of what you will say to each response.

You might have a few questions ready about the company or some interesting ways others in the industry have benefited from your product or service. If the person can't talk at the moment, ask when you can call next week or if there is a better time to call. Remember to be as gracious as possible, as we all have gotten calls from people at the wrong time. Put yourself in the other person's shoes. Above all, be friendly, courteous, and respectful. The person may be busy now, but later on when you call, when the person needs something you have, he or she will probably show a much warmer side.

Using E-mail as a Follow-Up

Sometimes you might have access to the e-mail address of the person with whom you have just spoken on the phone. It's always good to have something ready to e-mail over to the person after a phone call. By the way, you can always get the e-mail, do your research, do an online search, and go to the Web site. Be resourceful.

This is just one more way you can keep your name in front of them. Of course, use e-mail to confirm appointments that you've set up. Make sure you e-mail a week before to make contact, and then try to contact the person again the day before the meeting to confirm. You might even e-mail an article from the paper or a Web site that would be appropriate for your new contact. If you weren't able to talk very long on the phone with the person, you can also send a follow-up e-mail thanking the person for the time he or she did give you. Then, while your call is still fresh in the person's mind, elaborate briefly—only one paragraph at most—on why you were calling and what action you would like the person to take. You might ask for more information about how vendors are selected or what the person does when he or she needs a custom solution in your specialty area. Sometimes you can even get appointments set up through e-mail, or the person might forward you to his or her assistant who will book you an appointment via e-mail.

Person to Person

This can often be the hardest area for the introvert. However, whether you are an accountant, dentist, author, or artist, personal marketing is the key to giving what you have to give to a world that needs it. Personal marketing is about putting your best foot forward in front of other people.

We've already mentioned many of the challenges and strengths you possess as an introvert. You're known in your field for your expertise through your written articles and personal publicity. You've maximized your introvert traits by using an opener letter and e-mail to make good contacts. You've done your phone work and now, here you are, face to face with your contact. Perhaps this is a sales presentation, a "meet and greet" where your company comes in and does a presentation on your products or services, or a networking event where by "chance" you've run into your contact. Regardless, now is the time to really connect with others in the most personal of ways, face to face.

The important thing is to be yourself. That's right, you can only be one person, and that's yourself! People will see right through anything else. You certainly know what I mean because you can see right through others who pretend to be what they're not. Just put your best foot forward and let those ideas and goals come out, and you'll be surprised at how positive a response you get from others when they see your passion for what you are doing. Remember, you do have good ideas and want to help people where you can. You're a giver and you want the opportunity to serve. You are naturally the internalizer. Your gift is to take situations and challenges, process them from within, and create new paradigms for the outside world to use. Even though introverts make up just 25 percent of the population, the other 75 percent of the population needs what you can contribute, whether they always realize it or not! Let them know who you are and what you can contribute, and I believe you'll eventually see all your thoughts and dreams come to life.

Even if the people you meet are not an exact match for what you do in business, focus on them and give them the dignity and respect they deserve. You may have to politely break conversation and move on in your networking, but you'll have connected with the person and feel good about it. This respectful treatment of others will come back to you in many ways. Believe me, as I've told the story before, when I, as an introvert, first came to New York City twenty-plus years ago, I knew no one. Now I have more than forty-five hundred contacts in every realm of life and business, all of whom would (I hope) accept my call.

Small Talk for Introverts

The biggest challenge for most introverts in face-to-face communication is small talk. I have even seen coffee mugs on introvert discussion sites that exclaim, "I hate small talk!" Yet, this need not be the case. Small talk is simply the social lubricant that gets conversations started.

We've all been in group discussions where the speaker comes up with an icebreaker to get people talking. This is all small talk is, only it's in the context of two individuals instead of a group. Some introverts think there is something wrong or less than honest in making small talk. This need not be the case. You can make small talk with people while holding on to your integrity. Just be honest when you speak and respectfully withhold your opinion if you disagree. Most people won't press you too hard to agree with them when you're first getting to know them. If they do, and you are uncomfortable, simply excuse yourself politely and find someone else to talk with. What I am describing here is maybe one percent of the people you run into. The other 99 percent will be just as anxious as you are to make good connections and learn something as well.

Of course, there are some practical tips that are especially helpful for the introverted networker. We've mentioned earlier using a script. This can be a huge help for the quieter networker and will give you something to get the conversation started. For the introvert I also suggest having a few questions or comments ready as conversation starters.

Extroverts tend to have an easier time finding things to talk about. Introverts will want to map these out in their head beforehand. An example of a mental list would be:

1. Ask what they thought of the speaker tonight.

2. Ask why they came to this particular event.

3. Ask how this event compares to others they have been to that are similar.

Remember that 75 percent of the people you talk to love to talk. All you have to do is ask a few questions, and the conversation will flow on and on and they'll walk away thinking you're a brilliant conversationalist. And, the fact is, because you're such a good listener, you are! And you will have learned some new things along the way.

Of course, be ready with your thirty-second infomercial when they ask you about yourself. If you sense they are truly interested in what you are saying, be bold and let them see your passion, whatever it might be. This can be a great way to go from the small talk stage to really forming a personal relationship with someone.

Partnering with Extroverts

One way to capitalize on the natural skills of quieter networkers is to encourage them to partner with one of your more extroverted team members at networking events. The extrovert will naturally be good at making introductions and getting the conversation going. While this is happening, your introvert has picked up on the mood of each person, analyzed what the potential is for doing business, and is thinking about how he or she can solve the potential customer's problem. When the conversation naturally reaches the point where a solution is needed, it's time for the introvert to take the stage. The extrovert will need to defer to the introvert as the "expert" and move out of the way. This is especially effective at business events when engaging companies that you'd like to do business with, but have never interacted with before.

Tag Team Sales Call

Back from a sales call, Steve and Bill had totally different takes on what happened.

Steve, the extrovert, walked into the manager's officer saying, "What a great call! We aced it! They're definitely going to go forward with the proposal." Bill, on the other hand, looked puzzled as he expressed the opposite point of view and scratched his head in bewilderment. He was thinking, "Did I actually just participate in the same meeting Steve did?" Of course he did—what happened was that these two people looked at the meeting in completely different ways.

When Steve was telling the client, Rochelle, all about their suggested proposal, he was talking without listening as much and was not paying attention to details or body language. He was only focused on what he was saying, not on the nonverbal gaze he was getting from Rochelle. Bill, on the other hand, paid close attention to Rochelle and saw how she stiffened every time Steve blurted out another claim about why their product was the best and why they had to move forward. Bill watched her get interrupted if she tried to speak until she finally sat in total silence waiting for the meeting to end. Because her style was also that of an introvert, she smiled and said thank you and, as she ushered them to the door, said she would think about it, and that she had to dash off to another meeting.

Steve interpreted the meeting as a definite sale, where Bill saw it as a definite no-go. What could each of them have done differently to help the other and create a winning situation? Steve needed to carry his intangible tool kit—he needed to bring his ears and eyes. If he had observed Rochelle's body language, stopped talking, and started listening, he could have asked open-ended, high-gain questions.

Bill, on the other hand, with his strong intuitive and detail skills, saw what was happening. If he could have jumped in at the appropriate time to save his colleague by asking a question or giving a fact based on the research he had done before the meeting, he could have turned the meeting around. He was totally organized before he left the office and had a script in place, complete with potential objections and answers.

Steve and Bill needed to prepare before the meeting, go over the possible scenarios to decide what to do, and look at the situation from both vantage points. "Tag team" meetings with opposite personalities can produce amazing results. Each person sees the situation differently and, with some preparation and time management, together they can work wonders.

Look at your own situation; then go to your next meeting with one of your extroverted colleagues and plan in advance.

Write down and discuss your strengths and areas in which each of you is challenged. After the meeting debrief each other on what did or didn't happen and how you can move forward and learn from each other.

Recharging for Introverts

You might be thinking that all of this talk about personal marketing is starting to wear you out. That's okay! It's just the way you're wired.

Introverts need to take time to recharge and not feel guilty. Remember, you are processing things at a much deeper level than most people do. This is your strength, but it's also a great challenge because you will need the time to disengage from your external environment to give your internal self time to think, resolve, and rest.

The lunch meeting can be a great time to get business done. I recommend using mealtimes as often as possible to get to know people. This is one way we humans really connect with each other—by eating together. "Let's get a coffee" is also a very effective way to take things from the purely business to a more personal level. However, if you're an introvert, you need to plan some time for yourself throughout the day, if possible. If you can do this over lunch with a good book, great! If you need to use your lunches to conduct business, then I strongly suggest using a couple of ten-minute breaks in the morning and afternoon to recharge. They can be spent simply reading a weekly magazine, going for a quick walk, or even taking a short power nap (five minutes)—I don't want anyone getting fired for napping at work! Some more progressive companies are even creating nap or relaxation rooms for their employees to decompress. You may not think you have the time to do these things, but in the end you'll get more done every day by keeping yourself recharged.

Quiet, Yet Quite Successful

As I have tried to stress, even though introverts account for the minority of society, they have the potential to make some big-time contributions to the world. Their natural ability to process things internally and their great listening skills make them valuable assets to any team or business, especially when teamed with extroverts who know and value their abilities.

Introverts' intrinsic desire to have things organized and to have a plan can often set them apart from the crowd and, in time, make them very successful at whatever they set out to do. For many introverts, writing is a hidden talent they need to take advantage of. Writing out lists for assignments, names of various contacts, a networking plan—are all safe and comfortable activities for introverts. Then they can sit down by themselves, review the lists, and evaluate their next steps in connecting with people face-to-face. Remember to use your

While visiting my lifelong friends, Trudy and Bill, who are also my godparents, I was reminded again of the networking strengths of both extroverts and introverts. Trudy meets and greets, talks, and is friendly to everyone. She's also the first to stand up and give a short speech. Bill, conversely, is content visiting with a few people and having a conversation. He sometimes looks as if he's holding court when people gather around him waiting to hear what he will say, because what he says is important. He is intelligent and articulate. Together they're a powerful couple and both are superb networkers, yet each would say, "I'm not a networker. I'm just being who I am." Of course, this is the key. They both have superb interpersonal skills that have brought them a lifetime of friends and contacts.

internal passion to your advantage in person-to-person conversations. People love to talk with someone who is passionate about something they are also passionate about. Always stretch yourself, while honoring who you are, and take a break now and again to recharge. That way, you'll be your best for yourself and for others. Now you know a lot about yourself or your introverted co-worker, associate, or client. In the next chapter we focus in on how to use follow-up to make your network really thrive.

Exercise: Networking Self-Test for Introverts

1. Introverts have natural strengths that they bring to the business environment. Put a check next to your top strengths:

_____ Strategy and organization ability

_____ Problem solving ability

_____ Reading, writing, listening skills

_____ Making conversation in areas I am passionate about

_____ Caring for other's needs in a selfless way

_____ Other strength(s): _____

_____

■ The top three ways I can maximize my strengths in my current work week are: (Be sure to add these to your planner's task list!)

_____ Developing an "Introvert Networking Plan" for myself

_____ Finding ways to partner with extroverts when possible

_____ Develop "Opener Letters" before cold calling

_____ Writing scripts to use on the phone

_____ Utilizing e-mail networking

_____ Contributing articles to publications and websites

_____ Using thank you notes to let people know how much I care

_____ Providing the most thorough solutions for my customers' needs

_____ Other: _____

_____

2. Having inventoried your strengths as an introvert, it's time to grow those areas that are a challenge. Place a check next to the top three areas/situations that you would like to improve:

   ____ Small talk

   ____ Cold calling on the phone

   ____ Company parties

   ____ Networking events

   ____ Staff meetings

   ____ Client meetings

   ____ Making eye contact

   ____ Maintaining good posture

   ____ Maximizing writing strengths

   ____ Following up leads

   ____ Building in "recharge time" into my day

3. Next develop a "Learning Plan" to overcome these. I plan to stretch myself this year in the following three ways:

   a. _____

   b. _____

   c. _____

"Each player must accept the cards life deals him or her. Once they are in hand, he or she alone must decide how to play the cards in order to win the game."
—Voltaire

CHAPTER 7

Follow-Up: A Road Map for Growth

"Avoid shortcuts. They always take too much time in the long run."
—**Anonymous**

After any event, as I am walking out, I have an exit strategy in place for building my network. I'm ready to input information about new people I've met into my contact database, write follow-up notes, send any articles I've promised, and get the telephone numbers of at least two people to call and set up meetings with. We might be masterful at working the room and making contacts (though introverts and extroverts do it differently); however, without follow-up, one thing is certain. Nothing will ever happen.

Over and over I hear people say, "I was going to follow up, but I got so busy!" Or "I wasn't sure if the contact I made really meant for me to contact him." Whatever the excuse, if I've learned anything about finding, growing, and keeping contacts, it's that follow-up is the key to growing your network and your business. What we remember has a way of being rewarded.

Four "Must-Dos" After a Meeting

After any event or meeting, you will have a number of opportunities to follow up quickly and efficiently, based on conversations you had and contacts you made. Timing is of the essence. Tomorrow you will only have more things to do and more excuses for not doing them, so do it now.

1. Within twenty-four hours after a meeting, send a note or e-mail, or call to say any of the following, depending on the circumstances of your meeting:

- "It was nice to meet you." I was at an association dinner party recently where one of the guests, Nick, was sharing some information about his company. Even though we met and chatted only as we were walking out the door, I sent him a note the following day, telling him how much I had enjoyed meeting him and hearing his presentation. He responded, and we have met several times since. He let me in on two new opportunities, and we have formed a friendly business relationship.

- "Thank you for your time and consideration." Anyone who knows me or has heard my advice knows that I strongly believe in the power of the handwritten note. Here's how the power of a note can work: After a long day of meetings and interviews with the partners of a company where I was presenting a proposal for management coaching, I left armed with my note cards. Two days later, everyone received a personal note from me, thanking him or her for taking the time to meet with me. As it turned out, I didn't get the project, and was told I was a "close second." So, I sent each of them another note saying, "Thank you for your time and consideration" and expressing my hope that our paths might cross again. Some people might think that was a lot of work because I didn't get to close the deal. Yet it paid off, because a couple months later, I was called back in to do a more extensive project with some of the organization's internal people and created a strategic alliance to work with some of its clients. You never know how your thank-you notes will work. The personal note tells the client or prospect that you took the time to write, which will make you stand out.

- ■ "Perhaps we can meet again." When I speak with people, I always ask how it might be best to follow up. Remember, at various networking events your goal is to establish rapport and ask for permission to meet again. This was the case when I attended a huge industry event not long ago. I started chatting with the woman sitting to my left at lunch. Shortly into our conversation, it was time for the program to begin, and she had to dash out. She didn't have her card, so I wrote down her name and her company and then went to the company Web site and e-mailed her the next day, suggesting we meet for breakfast the following week. We did; I was able to hook her up with a new supplier, and she is now a new contact for me.

- ■ "Thank you for the useful information." While I always practice this suggestion, I have to say how nice it is to be on the receiving end! Recently I received several nice notes and e-mails after giving a short presentation at an event. I remember one in particular that came the next day, right in my e-mail box with the subject line, "Thank you for sharing some helpful thoughts." I always remember the people who follow up with me to say thanks or tell me that my information was helpful. We all like to hear this. Take the time today to think about someone who has recently given you some useful information—whether the person is an existing contact or someone you met recently—and drop him or her a note or e-mail to say so. Doing these follow-ups is more than courteous; it distinguishes you from the other people your contact has met.

2. If you have promised to send materials, call to set up a meeting, or pass on a referral, keep your word and do it within the time promised—or sooner. It's easy to make these promises at a meeting or event, but it is the person who follows up in a timely manner who is remembered and trusted.

3. Call within two weeks after suggesting a get-together, whether over a meal or at a more formal meeting. "Let's do lunch" is just an old cliché, unless you make it happen. Only suggest it if you mean it, and then follow up to set a specific date and place. And remember to call or send an e-mail to confirm the day before. Things happen in life, and people appreciate it when you take the time to do this added courtesy. If they must cancel, you'll have an opportunity to make other plans. Either way, you come across as being sincere and professional.

4. When a contact provides you with a referral or offers to pass on your information to help you out, be sure to say thank you and keep your contact in the loop by letting him or her know the results, whatever happens. The same holds true for any tangible advice you get from a contact. People who offer to help you, and then go out of their way to do it, deserve to know the results of their advice. And they certainly deserve a thank you! Again, these people are some of your advocates—they are helping to market you, and I consider them my "clients," too.

Several months ago when I spoke to a group about this subject, Jane, who had invited me, said, "Andrea, I must share a story, because as you are explaining the importance of this simple courtesy, I am seething with anger regarding a recent situation." She told me that her husband had referred their friend, Bill, for a project at her husband's client's company. They heard nothing from Bill until several months later at a party

AFTER YOUR FIRST MEETING

A gentle touch is often required as a follow-up with people we have just met. First and foremost, take the time to build rapport. If you have met someone new and then the next day you ask to set up a sales call or ask for a referral, you risk coming across as aggressive and self-centered and may damage a developing relationship. Remember to ask for permission to stay in touch. Send a note first, saying how much you enjoyed meeting the person and suggesting another meeting.

As I was waiting for my dinner guest one night at a restaurant, the woman in the next booth and I struck up a conversation. It turned out she had been a speaker at an event I had attended. I'd thought she was very interesting and insightful. I began discussing a few of the things I remembered from her talk, and we were still talking when our respective dinner partners arrived. I sent her a note the following day and a copy of my first book. She called me soon after and invited me to give a speech for her organization. Follow up!

when a mutual acquaintance told them that he had gotten the project. Never once did Bill thank them for the referral, let them know how the project was going, or even have the courtesy to let them know he had been successful. Jane was angry about Bill's rudeness after her husband had gone out of his way to help him. Some weeks later, she called me to say that Bill had recently left a message on her husband's machine asking if he could help out a "friend"—yet there was still no thank you! Needless to say, no further help was offered.

We have probably all been in situations like this where people forget their most important client, advocate, or referral source. Be sure to avoid those kinds of mistakes and take the time right now to repair any inadvertent damage you may have done. Dig deep and go back through your entire database.

Doing these follow-ups is good manners, helps build solid relationships for the future, and shows respect for others. "Respect" is the key word here. Remember, people do business with those whom they know and respect. They will want to help you again when the opportunity arises.

Thank-You Notes

As I have said, one of the best follow-up techniques is a simple thank-you note. It seems so obvious to thank someone, yet many people fail to do so. A handwritten note clearly makes you stand out and separates you from the others. At the very least, send off an e-mail or pick up the phone after your meeting just to say thanks, and you'll begin to build a relationship. Not long ago, when I sent a new contact a handwritten note, he responded to me by saying, "I know I shouldn't have been surprised, yet in this day and age of everything electronic, your note certainly made an impact."

Eight reasons to send a thank-you note are:

1. **For time and consideration.** This is one of the four "must dos" after a meeting, and also applies to many other situations such as interviews, one-on-one meetings, and even certain social encounters.

2. **For a compliment you received.** I met a woman at an event who had one of the most amazing pens I had ever seen. It was a great conversation starter. She told me it was her "signature piece" and she loved it. I sent her an article that I saw on pens, and she sent me a note written with her special pen thanking me for the compliment!

Recently, I found out that Dave, a former client of mine, had left his company to pursue another passion. I sent him a note, thanking him for all of his help in coordinating our projects and making my work so easy at his company. I also sent thank-you notes to the senior people with whom Dave used to work, in addition to his former assistant. Over the next two months, there was a flurry of activity at the company. I came up on the radar screens of all the people I'd contacted, which came from my "thank you" to each of them. So, as you can see, it's important to take the time to write these notes because they'll pay off over time.

THE TWO NEW "RS": RAPT ATTENTION AND REAL WRITING BY ANITA R. BRICK

While communication is quicker, easier, and much more mobile these days, it seems that far less of our message is actually heard. I receive so much junk mail and spam that I want to scream. I often ignore those senders and give my attention (and money) to people and organizations that write sincere messages with thought and care, targeted specifically to me. From my research and discussions with business executives in my role as Director of MBA Career Advancement Programs at the University of Chicago, Graduate School of Business, I know I am not alone.

Individuals are trying to stand out in order to advance their personal and organizational goals. They are spending enormous amounts of money and pushing and shoving each other to get a moment in the spotlight, yet many miss the point, because people want to be noticed and acknowledged in positive ways. So if you give them your rapt attention (i.e., single mindedly focusing on the other person) you will likely gain theirs, be remarkable, and make your goals a reality.

(continued on page 175)

3. **For a piece of advice given.** A client called me to offer her advice on how to design an upcoming presentation for some decision makers in her company. She spent quite a bit of time with me, so I immediately sat down and wrote her a thank-you note for her time and help.

4. **For business.** This is a "must do!" Every time someone does business with you or gives you an order, drop the person a thank-you note. Remember, someone else could have gotten that business instead of you. And remember also to send a thank-you note to all of those who were responsible for making the decision. Too often people only thank the top person; however, most decisions are made with input from many people. Be sure to send a note to everyone who was part of the decision. This will show your appreciation and reinforce your name with others in your client's business. It also strengthens what I call "surrounding the account," where you expose your potential client to your name and business on as many fronts as possible.

5. For a referral. After I spoke at a real estate company, one of the agents in the audience referred me to one of his clients. I sent him a note immediately. He continually tells me how much he appreciated that simple note. When you thank in writing the people who go out of their way for you, it guarantees you will stay on their radar screen.

6. For a gift. I read a wonderful story about a little girl who learned the power of thank-you notes when she was only seven. She thanked her mom and grandmother for every gift she received, often with a little drawing or card. Once she was so excited about the unique toothbrush her grandma gave her that she wrote up a little note saying she would think of her grandma every night when she brushed her teeth with her new toothbrush! You may be smiling—this kid is bright. Who do you think is remembered and rewarded all the time?

7. For help on a project. I am one lucky person. For this project—the book you're reading—I have had the amazing help of many great people, including Tom, a genius who works with me on my marketing; Kathleen, my incredible publisher; Duane, who is an amazing process man; Ian,

---

THE TWO NEW "RS"

(continued from page 174)

A simple and easy way to accomplish this is to send "Professional Love Notes"—handwritten notes of thanks, acknowledgment, or encouragement. This brings us to "Real Writing", which is genuine, sincere, and specific. Now this type of writing is not a "one size fits all" form letter where you keep the words, change the name, and you're set to go. "Real Writing" takes thought, time, and effort and is highly valued. If you don't know what to say, start by writing down why you want to thank or acknowledge a specific person. The basic things you might say out loud will often work, and the effort is appreciated much more than the exact wording. It's largely a matter of practice. The more you do it, the more confident you will become. No need to be perfect. Be sincere, authentic, and humble.

Writing Professional Love Notes℠ is one of the best investments you can make in your business and your life.

who is a bright young star; and Margaret, who is a great writer and interpreter. Although I send them notes continually thanking them for their help and insight, I want to publicly thank them again: "Without all of your help, this book would still be in my head!"

8. **Even when you are "rejected."** The door is never shut. My mantra is, always thank people for their time and consideration, even if nothing comes of it, because sometimes it does! And you can always learn something. One of my clients told me how her rejection of a consultant turned into an offer. When the first candidate she chose for the project didn't work out, she looked again at those with whom she'd met. She recalled one consultant who had sent a note thanking her for her consideration, despite the rejection letter he got. She called him in for another meeting and subsequently hired him for the project.

"When someone does something well, applaud! You will make two people happy."

—Samuel Goldwyn

My Thank-You Chain

I've mentioned my thank-you chain before and how I often use it to thank everyone who has helped me along the way. It's a simple, efficient, and powerful way to follow up and be remembered. I have thank-you chains throughout many companies where I work. For instance, I was giving a speech at an association meeting, and I met three new people who hired me for projects. The first thank you went to the organizer of the association meeting, and the others went to all of the people I knew from the group. I also sent over a basket of goodies because, without them, I never would have met these people. I have done several projects at one of the companies and continue to thank my original and secondary contacts, so the thank-you chain can grow.

I even have a system for my thank-you chain. I track every single opportunity back to the first introduction. I put this information into my database so that I can easily go back and see how the connection began. I thank all of the people in my chain by phone, e-mail, or note, depending on their preferred method of communication. People are often surprised by my thank you because they may not realize the part they played in the chain. It's fun to tell them how it evolved and that if it hadn't been for them, I would not have had this success. And I thank them!

Building Trust

People do business with those they trust and respect. Trust is the key word, and building trust takes time and patience. When we network, we need to learn to respect others' timetables. Often new contacts do not respond in a timely

YOUR PERSONAL THANK-YOU CHAIN

Working from present to past, think about the chain of events and people who led you to your current job (business, profession, or a major client). Make a list of the people who helped you through referrals or in other ways. Write, call, or send each of them an e-mail to thank them. Start by asking yourself:

1. How did I get my current job?

2. How did I get into this industry?

3. How did I meet my last two major clients?

THE POWER OF NINE

Every day I go through my database and do the following:

1. send three handwritten notes,

2. send three additional e-mails, and

3. make three additional phone calls.

My database includes people's names and their preferred means of communication ("E" for e-mail and "V" for voice mail), so I can say thank you or just touch base in the way they prefer. When combined with my personal notes, this becomes a powerful and effective way to maintain meaningful business relationships. It only takes about sixteen minutes of your day, and it's very "net-worth" it!

fashion—at least it seems that way. They may be busy with their own deadlines and have many responsibilities that keep them from responding to you immediately. So how can we move the process forward without "pushing" other people too hard, which will only make them more reluctant?

If someone you've met does not call back after being given a great introduction or offer, avoid badgering the person with follow-up calls. These are the types of calls that try to disguise the real question: "I think it's time that my efforts to get some business out of you paid off," or "What's taking you so long to respond to me?" Doing this will ruin any chances you have of developing a positive relationship.

These types of calls can best be avoided when earlier conversations include a couple of productive questions, such as, "How do you prefer to learn about new suppliers?" or "What is the best way to present product information to you?" This way you make it easy to do business with you, and you ultimately receive the response you're looking for.

Rushing a communication by hurrying off the phone or sending correspondence that is not carefully written—can become another networking stumbling block. It tells the new contact that you're trying to move through the process in a cold and mechanical way. Even when we have long lists of people to contact, it takes very little effort to develop a personalized approach. Here are three ways to do it:

- Ask your contacts how they want the issue to be handled and how they prefer to communicate. Some people prefer that everything be done in writing, while others would rather receive a quick follow-up phone call or e-mail, letting them know about new opportunities that can benefit them. This is so simple, yet watch how many of our calls elicit no response.

However, when we e-mail them, the response is immediate. We have just learned to communicate with people the way they like.

- Check on new contacts regularly. Salespeople are often told to deal with people quickly without having a long-term, follow-up plan in place. In fact, the long-term follow-up is more important. Mark your calendar for the next significant date on your contact's calendar. You can phone or e-mail a month before sending new information or material or even mention that you hope to connect with him or her at an upcoming conference or meeting.

- Develop a networking game plan. New contacts will never develop into anything important unless you have a long-term plan in place for keeping in touch with them. Keep a readily available list of all contacts. Using that list, develop a plan that is appropriate for all the contacts and choose which ones should receive special treatment. For instance, you may see that an effective follow-up strategy with a key contact may be looking for him or her at an upcoming business function. Another contact might appreciate a note with helpful information. Once you find out which method is most effective with each of your contacts, build on what works and develop the skills you need, such as writing and speaking, to make meaningful connections with those people.

Remember that the true key to growing your network is follow-up. Now that you have an expanding network, you need to figure out how to keep it alive. In the next chapter, we check out some great strategies for staying in touch with your contacts. Before you move on, try these quick exercises to help you follow up and grow your network!

Exercise 1: Eight Ways to Say "Thank You"

Look at the following eight reasons for sending a thank-you note. Next to each reason, write down at least one name of someone to whom you can write a thank-you note this week.

1. For time and consideration

_____

2. For a compliment you received

_____

3. For a piece of advice given

_____

4. For business

_____

5. For a referral

_____

6. For a gift

_____

7. For help on a project

_____

8. For considering you or your services even when you've been rejected.

_____

Exercise 2: Other Notes

There are other types of notes you can send any time to stay in touch and be helpful. Write down at least one name of someone to whom you can write a note this week. Consider the following reasons:

FYI (For your information)

_____

Congratulations

_____

Nice talking to (or meeting) you

_____

Thinking of you

_____

Other

_____

Exercise 3: Whom Will You Help?

Think of people in your network whom you can help or provide with a connection, information, or a referral.

Write their names down and take action.

_____

_____

_____

_____

T—**T**ake the time to say thank you to someone.

H—**H**ave a plan of action to incorporate this strategy every day.

A—**A**rticulate your note or compliment with powerful language.

N—**N**otice something special about each person.

K—**K**eep in touch sincerely and in your own style.

Y—**Y**ou is the most important word when thanking someone; tell others what is special about them.

O—**O**rganize yourself so that this process becomes seamless.

U—**U**nderstand the power of a sincere and considerate thank you.

"Life is like a soap opera. God is the head writer; your story line keeps changing; it's a daily event; and there are Friday cliffhangers."

—Anonymous

"We are continually faced by great opportunities brilliantly disguised as problems."

—Lee Iacocca

"Small opportunities are often the beginning of great enterprises."

—Demosthenes

PART 3
KEEP:
Maintaining Your Hard Earned Relationships

"Imagination is more important than knowledge. Knowledge is limited. Imagination encircles the world." —**Albert Einstein**

Our final section is probably the most compelling because we can spend a lot of time finding and growing our business relationships using the powerful art of networking. However, in order to see that everything is running productively, we must make sure that we keep our business by retaining those amazing relationships.

We will focus on creative ways to cultivate advocates in our networking relationships and be aware of continually identifying potential opportunities to do so. You'll find out how to earn referrals for your business and to make sure that everyone on your team realizes they help bring in business or are "rainmakers," and must help keep the business you have. We will talk more about how to be proactive and stay in touch by remaining on our advocates' and clients' radar screens. You'll also learn how to manage all of this with your own database management system—whether you are in the office or on the road.

Finally, we will tie it all together and talk about how to make networking part of your DNA (Dedicated Networking Always). You will learn my ten easy-to-remember networking suggestions based on my acronym out of, what else—the word NETWORKING!

CHAPTER 8

Stay in Touch

> *"All of our
> dreams come true,
> if we have the courage
> to pursue them."*
> —**Walt Disney**

Following up in a timely manner with materials promised, an immediate thank you, or a "nice seeing you" note is a must for effective networking. The sure way to lose a contact is to fail to follow up and follow through. However, the next step is equally important, yet often neglected in today's busy world. This is the process of keeping in touch on a continual basis. Imagine how awkward it would be to contact someone you once met and ask for a favor if you haven't stayed in touch. This is an example of the kind of action that gives networking a bad name and makes people dislike these "What's In It for Me" types. Our surveys indicate that people are turned off by contacts who call or e-mail them only when they need something. If you stay in touch with your networking contacts and nurture your network regularly, you'll receive a much more positive response to future requests.

Ways to Stay on Your Contacts' Radar Screen

To keep a relationship going, you need to stay on your contacts' radar screen. Recently a friend mentioned to me that while it was easy for her to send an e-mail or a note after she met someone, it was much harder for her to stay in touch after that. Follow-up, she told me, is reacting to a situation that calls for a response or action on her part. However, when she heard my comment about staying on your contacts' radar screen, she asked me, "After the follow-up, what 'excuse' do I have to contact this person?"

"Sometimes," I told her, "you have to invent the opportunity (the word, excuse, gave me the hives!) and you have to vary the contact methods."

If follow-up is reactive, think of staying in touch as proactive. It involves looking for ways to stay in touch and building on the relationship, so that when an opportunity arises to ask for some advice, you can do it easily because you have a solid relationship. Here are some methods I use to stay on my contacts' radar screen.

Notes

Besides the thank-you note, which is a follow-up must, there are several other types of notes you can send at any time to stay in touch, be helpful, and be remembered. Since handwritten notes are so rare, yours will really make an impression.

- **"FYI" (For your information).** Send newspaper or magazine articles to people in your network, with a note saying, "I thought you might be interested in this." The articles can be related to the person's business or personal interests. I have a contact who is a huge Yankees fan, so I've sent him pictures from the Sunday newspaper and several articles on his favorite team. He's been appreciative of those, especially because I took the time to find out what he cares about. How did I remember what he likes? I wrote it all down, and now it's on my database under his name and information.

Another way you can give your contacts helpful information is by sending them information from a seminar you've attended or information about an upcoming conference or class. Any information that helps them understand the latest trends in their business is good, too, in addition to any helpful leads.

- **"Congratulations!"** Send a note of congratulations for a promotion, an award or honor, or an anniversary. I sent a former colleague a note of congratulations when I saw an article that a mutual contact, an editor we both knew, had written about him. I wrote them both, congratulating my colleague on his promotion and complimenting my editor friend on his great article. It was a good opportunity to reconnect with both contacts and helped us to keep in touch. My former colleague ended up hiring me for a project. He's a busy person, and although he might have considered me among others for his project, I clearly believe it was because we stayed in touch with each other. It made him think of me instead of my competition. Also, he is totally bottom line-oriented—his e-mails are never more than about ten words! I respond and write to him in exactly "his" way.

- **"Nice talking to (or meeting) you."** You can send these notes any time you speak with someone on the phone or at a meeting. I even send them after a chance encounter and conversation. I have some great note cards with a picture of a phone and "Nice talking to you" on the front. Use any technique you can think of to make you stand out from the crowd. I call this the power of "remember-ability." People are always amazed and it reinforces our discussion as well.

■ **"Thinking of you."** I've found that when I send this type of note to people with whom I've not been in touch for a while, it often reopens the relationship. Laney had been a student in a presentation skills class years ago when she was in advertising. We stayed in touch at her next job, and then she started her own business—in, of all things, greeting cards. Now I'm one of her best clients.

■ **"Wish you were here."** I send out postcards wherever I go. I travel quite a bit and have found that this is a great way to stay in touch with contacts when I'm away from my office. My good friend and client, Bob, always sends me postcards from his world travels. He has a great system. He prints labels from his mailing list and takes them with him. Then he just writes the card and sticks a label on it. Easy!

You may be wondering how I have the time to send handwritten notes. I always carry notes and stamps with me. I use the time in airports, on trains, waiting at the doctor's office, or watching television to dash off a note, address it, and drop it in the mail. All it takes is carrying note cards in your networking tool kit, keeping a supply of stamps on hand, and, of course, being organized.

Holiday Cards and Special Occasions

Sending seasons greetings cards to everyone in my network is a practice I have done for many years. I also send greeting cards on special occasions and other holidays. Many people throughout the world, for instance, celebrate Chinese New Year or the Jewish New Year (Rosh Hashanah), St. Patrick's Day, Mother's Day, or Veterans Day. I even send e-cards on

BENEFITS OF SENDING GREETING CARDS

The Greeting Card Association tells us that sending a greeting card is a simple yet powerful gesture that reminds people someone is thinking of them. When you make someone else feel good, it also makes you feel good!

People often ask me how I find out my contacts' birthdays. I just casually ask them what month they were born after I've known them for a while. Then I record it in my database. My contacts usually forget they've told me their birthday.

Chocolate Day if I know my clients like chocolate. Yes, there is such a thing as Chocolate Day!

Birthdays, anniversaries, and other important events are also opportunities to keep in touch with a note or small gift. Pay attention to what people mention about these dates. Some people are proud of work anniversaries, so you can send a note of congratulations on these occasions. Others mention an upcoming award, honor, or promotion. If you haven't heard about these important days from your contacts, you can find out about them from their co-workers or in articles. I've been collecting these days of importance for a while, and some months I send out as many as eighty personal greeting cards! My recipients continue to be surprised and happy to hear from me.

The key is to consider the profile and interests of your contact when sending a card. The card industry has millions of choices for you to give your contacts a little loving care—and to remind them of you.

Interesting E-mails

Even though a handwritten note is a unique and thoughtful way to stay in touch, e-mails can also make you stand out. They can be used for the same reasons as notes and you can use your own unique style to create them. Send links to interesting online articles and Web sites, inspirational quotes, pictures, and videos. You can also include articles, video clips, or pictures in the body of your e-mail, with a personalized, friendly note on top.

Another way to use e-mail to stay in touch is to let your clients know about any charity or community work you're doing. For instance, if your company is involved in a tutoring program, you can send an e-mail to your clients about it, along with your note and pictures.

There are many discussion forums and weblogs online that cover a wide range of topics; find some that would interest your client. Start the e-mail with something like, "I saw a discussion on this Web site about the distribution issues we were talking about. Thought you might be interested," and include the link to the Web site.

I also use e-mail to send monthly tips to people who have signed up for them at my Web site. Or you can include a signature at the bottom of your e-mail that says, "Click here to get monthly tips." Some people send out e-mails to their contacts every time their Web sites are updated with new information, products, or articles.

"If I have ever made any valuable discoveries, it has been owing more to patient attention, than to any other talent."
—Isaac Newton

STAY CONNECTED!

- Set aside a few minutes each day or week to reach out to others. A simple phone call, e-mail, or card reminds people you care.

- Take time to reflect on what is important and of value in your life. I started my own "gratitude and nice card file," where I put a note each time I think of something for which I am grateful. Doing this is also a way to remember the strong personal connections I've created.

- Connect and stay in touch—for any reason. Life is too short to wait for a "special day"; every day is special.

- Reflect your own personality when reaching out to people.

- Hold on to your personal connections through something tangible. This is why I have my "nice card file"—it gives me an opportunity to remember very special connections.

Whatever you do, just make sure you have a valid reason for sending e-mails and tailor your message to the recipient. Also remember to reply to e-mails within twenty-four hours of receiving, even if only to acknowledge that you've received them, and promise to reply in detail later.

Your Own Article or Newsletter

If you have published an article in a trade publication, newsletter, or online, send or e-mail a copy of it to your contacts with a personal note. If you have yet to get an article published, create your own. You can print it on nice stationery, e-mail a copy to your contacts, or post it on your Web site and e-mail your contacts the link.

I've compiled my articles into a newsletter with tips and techniques on networking, presentation skills, sales, and customer service. People in my network tell me they enjoy reading it, and it's a great way to stay in touch. When my list was smaller and I sent my newsletter through the mail, I personalized each one with a note. Today I send it electronically. It goes out to many more people now, and in the body of the newsletter I include a note reflecting what has been going on, along with my articles and tips. Since my list has grown quite a bit, I always ask people for their permission to send my newsletter and monthly tips, which are a good way for me to grow and keep these relationships.

People often e-mail me back about something they liked or acted on based on my newsletter or tip of the month. I always respond to each one with an e-mail to say thank you!

Gifts

Everyone enjoys a nice gift to celebrate a special occasion, such as the completion of a project, when someone is promoted, for a birthday or holiday, or when someone has done a special favor for me. Though sending a gift sets you apart, you need to be careful about the nature of the gift. Keep in mind that this is a gesture of appreciation and avoid placing the recipient in the awkward position of having to turn down your gift because of company policy. In general, food and flowers are good choices because the whole company can share them. I like to send a fruit basket, tin of popcorn, box of candy, or other goodies. Of course, when your food gift is shared with others in the company, your name gets in front of others—an added bonus.

GIVE A GIFT

G—Giving Gifts that make you memorable

I—Invite and Involve people in special events

F—Friendly people are giving people

T—Time Together with somebody

Make sure you consider the recipient's preferences and habits in deciding what gifts to send and respect people's diets. These days, I'm careful to avoid giving candy or popcorn to clients who are watching their carbohydrate counts! I'm always on the lookout for items that people will like and can accept. One workshop participant told me about sending a bouquet of flowers to a client to thank him for some business. It turned out he was allergic to flowers, so after finding out from his assistant that a plant was fine, he immediately got one with an apologetic note. I recorded his allergy in my contact database so I wouldn't make this mistake again.

I met one of my favorite vendors over the Internet when he e-mailed me to ask permission to use one of my articles in his newsletter. I was happy to do so and was in the market for a gift basket, so I tried it. (Pretty clever networking on his part!) Be creative with your food gifts. I've sent everything from chocolate telephones to fruit-flavored flowers.

Give the gift of a book that you like or one that has a special message. Send it with a note about why you thought your contact would also like it. People rarely throw away books; at the very least, they pass them along to someone else. My first book, *Nonstop Networking*, has been a great gift for me to give out and it has become my calling card. I also sign and personalize each copy. I've actually incorporated what I call "give away a book a day to keep your networking growing day by day." Every day I give or send one out as a gift to someone. I'm looking forward to making *Million Dollar Networking* my next calling card and my preferred method of staying on radar screens.

I give gift certificates where people can choose what they want—all they have to do is order it. The fact that you ordered it at a store they like will show them that you went the extra mile. You may find that e-coupons and gift certificates are more convenient to send, too. The important thing is to do what works for you and makes your clients happy and to keep it professional.

Premiums

Invest in premiums with your company's name: pens, notepad holders, magnets, and paperweights—anything useful and memorable. I give premiums to everyone who attends my seminars or to people I meet at events. Each premium has my name, company, and contact information, including my Web site. Most important, all my premiums are useful. My signature piece is a pocket mirror that says, "Can your smile be heard?" Every year I look for a new premium that will put my name in front of my contacts as they go about their working day. I love giving gifts that stay on people's desks. When they're functional, they are a constant reminder of your services.

Personalize each premium with a brief note and individualized message, just as you would for any gift.

Face Time

Despite the immediacy and efficiency of e-mail, phones, and faxes, spending personal time with a client is memorable and more powerful. It may seem difficult to find the time to get together because we're all busy and live far apart. However, if you are persistent and creative, you can schedule these all-important personal meetings. Besides the traditional breakfast, lunch, and dinner meetings, suggest meeting for coffee or afternoon tea. Coffee shops are always in vogue for

networking meetings. Or try playing a game of tennis or golf; going for a walk; meeting at a museum; getting a manicure; shopping; attending an industry event; or attending a play, concert, or sporting event. Share a cab to a meeting or meet at the sky club at the airport when you're between flights in your colleague's city. Before going on a business trip or vacation, look up everyone you know in the places you'll be visiting, then call or e-mail before going to arrange meetings. I had dinner recently in Atlanta with several business friends, found out they had common interests, and made a wonderful connection with each of them.

Everyone is busy, yet I still manage to spend time with people in my network. I meet with some people at least once a quarter and others a couple of times a year. I see closer associates and friends more frequently.

Because of my travel schedule, I like to become familiar with, and then recognized at, the better restaurants and hotels for entertaining clients. I often find these through recommendations from people in my network. After eating or staying there, I send the hotel or restaurant manager a thank-you note saying that I'll be visiting again in the near future. I have been happily surprised to receive very nice treatment when I return. Again, just showing appreciation and saying thank you have set me apart and made these people remember me.

Share Your Expertise

I have a friend who is a consultant and a magician. He is often asked to perform his magic show at charity events and gives his time willingly. He contributes to the cause through his magic, stays in touch with people in his network, and even meets some new contacts at these events. He always walks away from these events with new business. People see him in action and remember him. What better way to build name recognition?

Think of your own expertise. When you offer your writing, proof-reading, publicity, computer, organizational skills, or any of your business or personal skills, you'll experience the satisfaction of knowing that you are helping others. When you take some time out of your hectic schedule to help someone else, you never know when the favor will be returned. Others appreciate and seek out knowledgeable people who want to give generously of their expertise. And when you have been a resource to people, they are more than willing to help you when you ask. Just avoid keeping score; do it because you want to help instead of keeping track of what is owed to you. Again, that says "negative networking" to me.

A DAILY, WEEKLY, MONTHLY PLAN TO STAY IN TOUCH

1. Every day, send an e-mail to three people you haven't been in touch with for a while (or create variety with one note, one e-mail, and one phone call).
2. Once a week, go through your contact list and call three people just to say hello.
3. Once a month, have lunch with a friend, colleague, or client you haven't seen for awhile.

Simple Technology

Recently, more and more people are using videoconferencing, text messaging, and instant messaging because they are more cost-effective and convenient. Whether you're using e-mail or the phone or meeting face-to-face, decide what works best for you—and your contact—and what will make you stand out while maintaining meaningful personal contacts.

Setting Up and Managing Your Contact Database

Since I wrote about this topic in *Nonstop Networking*, I have become somewhat of a gadget enthusiast. However, I still keep my system simple, flexible, and usable for me. It's a part of my KISS theory (Keep It Simple Sweetheart). My system for organizing and keeping track of a network database will work on any system you have. I have a friend who says, "My life is in three Rolodexes in my office." It works for him, and he's very successful.

You can use any contact management application that works best for you. There are so many that I encourage you to consult with an expert or someone you trust to find out what might work best for you. The key for any type of contact management system is that you find one method that is easy to use and that you can use consistently. The best networkers use a system that's organized and accessible.

I now proudly use my PDA for phone numbers and addresses and keep my calendar on it as well. I coordinate it every day with my computer to keep up to date with my data entries. I also am a new fan of the hand-held e-mail device. Yes, I've been known to check my e-mail in the hair salon or grocery store or whenever there's an opportunity (except, of course, in meetings, at meals, or at events).

I also carry my cell phone. Now some may wonder why I carry three devices when I could have them all in one. While I agree that I could combine them, this system works best for me, and that's the bottom line. Find the system that works with your lifestyle and the technology with which you are comfortable.

Setting Up a Contact Database

I still use the same system that I talked about in *Nonstop Networking* because it has worked well for me. I keep all of the contact information on the people in my network, including an "E" or "V" for how they want to be contacted (e-mail or voice mail). In addition to any work-related notes, including notes from conversations we've had, I enter every bit of information I have found out about their interests, favorite places and things, families, and anything else, so I can customize how I keep in touch with them. I also keep track of what gifts and cards I've sent them and how they fit in my "thank-you" chain.

I prioritize my contacts by putting an "A," "B," or "C" next to their names (which I explain in the next section) to help me decide how often to follow up with them. I also note whether they're introverts or extroverts, so I remember how to best communicate with them.

I continue adding information and meeting notes with the dates they occurred to the notes section. This gives me a complete record of interactions I've had with each person in my database. I also track how I came to know each person—who introduced us and how, when and where we met. This is critical information for my "thank-you chain" contacts.

I back up the information on my database at least once a week. In addition to my computer's hard drive, I have backups on CDs and on an external hard drive. I never worry that my life will go up in smoke if something happens to my computer. Everything is backed up continually.

Prioritizing Your Network

My current database consists of more than forty-five hundred people— all of whom I have met or spoken with during my career. They have attended one or more of my workshops and seminars, are associates and colleagues of my business, or are personal contacts. They have all become part of my universal network.

I am frequently asked how I manage to keep in touch with all of the people on my networking list. First, the majority of the people in my database comprise my mailing list, and I reach them regularly with my newsletter or tip of the month.

I divide the rest of my list into three categories—A, B, and C—and I have a contact plan for each category. I organize all my contacts, professional and personal, in the same database because business opportunities can happen through different kinds of connections, and there's so much interchange and flow among various areas of my life.

My "C" list has people with whom I "touch base." These are casual acquaintances with whom I am not currently doing business. They may also be former clients or part of my "thank-you" chain. I e-mail each of them my newsletter and tip of the month, and I send them a card or note once or twice a year, plus a holiday card. There are currently about three hundred and fifty people on this list.

My "B" list has "associates" with whom I am actively involved. I find a way to meet everyone on this list in person at least twice a year for a meal or coffee. I also send them at least six personal notes a year. If we're unable to get together, I call them every other month. I also send them holiday and premium gifts, my newsletter, and a holiday card. There are about a hundred people in this list.

My "A" list is made up of close friends and associates. I see each of them at least four times a year for a meal or longer, if possible. I send them special gifts, holiday cards, and premiums, and I also frequently send them personal notes and articles. I look for opportunities to send flowers, theater tickets, or dinner certificates. I constantly think of ways to stay in touch with the forty people on this list.

As you can see, because my contacts are categorized, I'm very realistic about how I can stay in touch with them in a quality way. I'm thrilled to have a huge contact base, yet the majority of these people are my electronic buddies. They mostly receive my newsletter and tip of the month. People have moved from this list to become closer associates when we've been in touch, they have followed up with me, or I've reconnected with them at an event or function.

These categories change continually because my network grows every day. I add new people to the appropriate category and move people between the lists, depending on what happens in life and how different connections occur.

If there is a D list, it includes people who are no longer in my life, either for a period of time or forever. It's not personal. On the other hand, last year I reconnected with three people I knew from different venues eight, ten, and twelve years ago. They all reappeared at different times, and we just picked up where we left off. One of them has become a client, and I've been able to help another with a training plan for her company. I'm glad that all three are back in my life! That's one of the greatest parts of continual networking.

Birthdays

I keep track of birthdays by adding the contact's birthday month into the database. Then I create a birthday file in a simple MS Word file folder and make each month a separate document. Then, once a month, I print out the list and mail each person a birthday card. Recently, I've started to add anniversaries and other special dates in the appropriate months, so I have all the important dates in front of me and can send out my greetings. This makes it easy to remember. Plenty of software programs will do this for you; however, my low-tech system works for me.

Business Cards

The more you network, the more business cards you will collect, so you'll need a system to record all of that information. Here's what I do: when I get a card, I immediately add it to my database. Often I get a large stack of cards from people who simply want to be on the newsletter list. I go through these quickly, separate out the ones I made a connection with, and find an additional reason to follow up and say thank you. I send my follow-up notes and enter the information into my database, and I set the rest aside for my assistant to enter into the mailing database.

STAYING IN TOUCH WITH A NEW CONTACT

When you meet someone at an event, try the following:

- record the information from the business card in your contact database;

- enter the date, where you met and how (if it was through someone else), notes about the person's profession, family, and interests;

- record notes about your conversation;

- send a "Nice to meet you" note; and

- mark down in your PDA or calendar that you should call in two weeks for a follow-up meeting.

If the contact is going to become a client or prospect, I staple the card to a file folder in which I keep materials and other information. I put other cards into the "circular file" next to my desk since I've already captured the information in my database and I like things to be clutter free!

Conversations and Meetings

I take notes on all of the conversations I have, including business matters and important follow-up tasks and dates. I also enter any personal information, such as a favorite team, hobbies, or upcoming family celebrations. These notes serve as conversation starters for the next time we meet as well as reminders to send a note. I record all the notes in the "activities" section of the contact's record in my computer database, including the

A TYPICAL DAY

When I'm away from the office, I make sure to keep in touch with my network. Here is how I did this most recently when I was conducting an off-site workshop.

During each of the breaks in the day (excluding lunch, which was a meeting):

1. I checked phone messages and prioritized them to determine who had to be called immediately.
2. I returned the priority calls right away and returned the others within twenty-four hours.
3. I checked and responded to e-mails using my Blackberry.
4. I called a prospect who had been referred to me. We spoke briefly and set up a future phone appointment. This gave me a chance to check the prospect's Web site so I would be prepared when we spoke. I also e-mailed the referral contact (his preferred method) to say thank you and asked if there was anything I needed to know about the prospect. I wrote all of this in my notepad (I still write faster than I can use the stylus on the PDA).

(continued on page 203)

date, purpose of the meeting, highlights of our discussions, and follow-up tasks and dates. I make sure to have a running log of every contact and conversation and I always date them. Very often I also save our e-mail correspondence in a folder on my computer with the person's name and company so I have a complete information trail at my fingertips that is simple and organized. I also enter all the data into my digital organizer follow-up file.

On the Road

Because I travel a lot, I need to keep in touch with others wherever I am in the world. So I take my network with me by carrying wonderful, compact, high-tech portable devices. I used to carry my laptop everywhere. Now, even though I have a new compact laptop, I only carry it when I'm working on something where I absolutely need my computer, such as writing this book. I can also access all of my computer files through a "thumb drive" on which I have downloaded all the files from my office computer. It fits right into the USB port and is basically an external hard drive you can hold in your hand!

I always carry my PDA, which has my contact information and calendar as well as my follow-up files. I keep all of these files coordinated with my computer. If I enter data to my PDA while I'm on the road, I download it to my computer when I return. Likewise, if I enter data on my computer, I regularly "hot sync" it to my PDA so I always have the latest data on hand.

My latest addition is my handheld e-mail system. This is a wonderful compact device that eliminates the need for a laptop to check e-mail. It allows me to quickly send off an e-mail to someone if I will be in a meeting and want to speak with the person later. All of these devices keep me in touch and they all fit in my handbag!

I always have my cell phone with me, which has important contact numbers so I can make quick calls. I store other numbers in my PDA. As I mentioned before, you can buy one device that will do everything for you—e-mail, phone, calendar, and notes. I happen to like having separate devices. For instance, I can speak to someone on the phone who has just sent me an e-mail and, while I'm looking at his e-mail on my Blackberry, I can check the calendar on my Palm Pilot to arrange a future meeting. This works for me; find a system that works for you.

In the past few years, I have become much more technology-driven with my portable networking equipment. Again, find a system that works for you. Day planners are alive and well, and many people still love them. I say,

A TYPICAL DAY

(continued from page 202)

When I returned to my office, I did the following:

1. Sent the prospect a handwritten note.
2. Sent my referral source a handwritten note to thank him for the referral.
3. Entered all of the information into my database.
4. Visited the prospect's Web site and prepared for our phone meeting the next day.
5. Returned the rest of my phone messages.

"bravo," as long as you're using some sort of contact management and data-base system that will help you build your network.

A Game Plan to Stay in Touch

Decide how often you want to contact the people in your network. I review my contact list every month. It usually takes about three hours and I manage to do it by breaking it up into small blocks of time. First, I review every contact record to see if it is up to date and I make any category changes that are necessary. Then I print out the records for each of my A and B contacts. From this, I make a contact plan for the month. I deter-mine whom I need to contact, why, and when, and I mark it on my PDA. My goal is to list at least nine people to contact every day during that month. It's what I call, "The Power of Nine."

As I add new people to my database, within twenty-four hours I send them a "Nice to meet you" note or e-mail with a copy of my newsletter. My calendar has follow-up dates and tasks that become a part of my daily "to do" list, the names of the nine people I should contact, and any cards I should send.

Staying in touch with everyone in your network is an art and a science. People like to be remembered and contacted in thoughtful ways. However, as your network grows, you need to create a system for staying connected with so many people. The successful networker knows how to combine these two tasks to create a seamless networking fabric in their lives.

In the next chapter, we'll look at how to create your own "fan club," which involves building and maintaining a group of advocates who take it upon themselves to help you succeed in your business life.

Exercise 1: The Power of Three (or Nine)

The best way to stay in touch with people is to make a habit of contacting at least three of them a day by note, e-mail, or phone. This allows you to make staying in touch a part of your busy schedule. Beside each category below, write the name of at least one person to whom you will write a note, make a phone call, or send an e-mail. You can extend this exercise by writing up to three people's names for each day of the week. Make a copy of this form and do this exercise every day for a month to make it a habit!

Co-worker:

Prospect:

Client:

Friend:

Service Provider:

Family Member:

Note: I keep raising the bar for myself—and I have increased the Power of Three to the Power of Nine. Many of my colleagues and workshop participants have done the same.

Take small steps—Start with three a day and make it a part of your life.

"Inch by inch, it is a cinch—yard by yard, it is hard."
—Anonymous

Exercise 2: Strengthening Your Network

The longer a working relationship has been in existence, the stronger it gets. However, it takes effort to make that happen. The following questions will help you think about ways to build better and stronger connections with others.

What do you think are the three most effective ways to show appreciation after someone has given you business referrals?

1. _____

2. _____

3. _____

What are three important dates that most people celebrate that you can remember with a card or by making a phone call?

1. _____

2. _____

3. _____

What could someone do for you that would justify sending a thank-you gift? (List up to three.)

1. _____

2. _____

3. _____

"Kindness is a language the deaf can hear, the blind can see and the mute can speak."
—Anonymous

"Vision without action is a daydream. Action without vision is a nightmare."
—Japanese proverb

CHAPTER 9

Creating Advocates

> "Formulate and stamp
> indelibly on your mind
> a mental picture of
> yourself as succeeding.
> Hold this picture
> tenaciously and never
> permit it to fade.
> Your mind will seek to
> develop this picture."
>
> **—Dr. Norman Vincent Peale**

One afternoon last fall, I received a phone call from a representative of the Executive Woman's Reading Council of a large bank informing me that my book, *Nonstop Networking*, had been chosen as its book of the month. After I thanked the caller, I asked her how she heard about my book. I knew that I could have called and sent copies of my book to the council for months, without any success. So why was my book selected? I had an advocate! Erinn, a young woman whom I met and helped several years ago, now worked for a member of the selection committee and had recommended my book. As Erinn later wrote me, "I never forgot how you helped me when I was out of work, meeting me for a soda at the diner, listening, and offering your advice. You don't know how much I appreciated it." Well, I do, and I'm thankful that Erinn is my advocate!

In business, networking is a necessary skill for finding and developing new clients and keeping those you have. It's also an opportunity to create advocates for your business. These advocates will be your best sales and marketing champions because they know and respect you. They will talk about you and your business in a positive way. This is a credibility factor that no one can buy—it comes from working hard and smart to create powerful connections.

Recently, I received an e-mail with the subject line, "You come highly recommended." It was from the executive vice president for human resources of a large holding company, asking for a meeting to discuss my training programs. As I read the e-mail, I saw that a former client had referred me. Even with both of our crazy schedules, we manage to keep in touch with each other in person or by e-mail and notes. In fact, we had met for breakfast not long before. After our breakfast meeting, he told a colleague about me and I then received the e-mail requesting a meeting.

Of course, even when we do have our advocates, we still need to sell ourselves directly to our prospects and clients. When our advocates open the door for us, we must stay in there and close the deal. It pays to create these advocates who believe in us and who can leverage our marketing efforts.

Identifying Potential Advocates

The Satisfied Client

Who can be better advocates than satisfied clients? They can give testimonials and refer you to others. Sometimes we may feel awkward about asking for referrals; however, there are ways to make asking easier. I had just finished a project at a new company where I had gotten to know several people quite well. While we were talking during our celebration lunch, I said, "As we debrief, tell me what you liked best about our program." It was a positive discussion, and I thanked them all. Then I said, "I'd be happy to work with anyone you feel comfortable referring me to." Two weeks later, I received a call from a colleague of one of the people at the luncheon asking me for an appointment to learn about my services.

Another time, I was referred to the former boss of a person I had worked with on a project. When Natalie called me, she said that Allison, who used to work for her, recommended me to do the same project for her organization. Of course, I thanked both Natalie and Allison and kept Allison in the loop as the project progressed. Your advocates stay with you when you stay in touch! This is part of the "Thank-You Chain" I talked about in chapter 7.

Good times to ask satisfied clients for referrals are after a success, when you are meeting during a social gathering, and when you have solved any problems that have occurred.

People You Work with: Your Team

Whatever someone's job description may be, it is ultimately a sales job. You may be thinking, "Wait—my assistant doesn't sell. What does sales have to do with that type of job?" Anyone who has a client contact, whether a direct one, as in sales and customer service, or indirect, as in production or accounting, is ultimately responsible for selling and marketing the company. You need to help everyone around you think like this. Your assistant may speak all day to your clients, internal support teams, and your management. The way he or she communicates directly reflects on you. You should empower your team members to think of ways to create and develop more business opportunities, regardless of their job function.

If everyone on your team could think, "How is what I'm doing helping the client—whether internal or external?" then everyone would

Too often people only "network" up the corporate ladder. My theory is that every single person is important and is part of your internal team. Smart people know to build relationships and alliances with those up, down, sideways, and across. Create and build relationships throughout the company.

be an advocate for your company. Helping an internal client—co-workers who depend on you to help them get their jobs done—is as important as helping an external client. First and foremost, you must build and maintain a strong foundation.

Creating advocates in your company takes the same networking skills we have been discussing. Find out who you need in your network and get to know them—listen and learn. Then make the connection and stay in touch.

Contacts and Colleagues in Your Business or Industry

In today's specialized world, many of the contacts you make in your industry will refer business to you because you specialize in an area that is needed. Here is where your self-marketing skills will be necessary. Fine-tune your thirty-second infomercial, become known in your field by giving presentations and writing articles, join and participate in professional organizations, and follow up and stay in touch with your network contacts.

If you read my first book, you know about a woman I know who launched her photography business. Several years later, she has a successful portrait studio. Much of her business comes from referrals from other photographers who specialize in commercial work. They refer their clients to her for portraits and executive head shots, and she refers clients to them for catalogs and brochures. She is a specialist in her area and has a reputation as being one of the best. The key here is to identify what you do best and to make sure that becomes your "brand," so that when people need what you do, you'll pop up on their radar screen.

Others at Your Client's Place of Business

It's important to reach beyond your comfort zone and meet more people, develop more relationships, and learn that even with your strongest business accounts, it is critical to "surround the account" and know several people at the firm or organization.

At one firm with which I work, Linda used to be my main contact, Claudette was her assistant, Alice worked next to her, and David and Michael were assistants. By creating and developing relationships with all of these people and staying on their radar screens, I have expanded my network and have set the scene for more business. Recently, Linda left the company and went to another. I kept in touch with her and will be presenting a proposal to her new company soon. Claudette, her assistant, was promoted, and because of my relationship with her and others, I have kept my business at that company.

Several years ago, I helped Carol find a new job, then she introduced me to the decision makers in her company, who hired me to do a training program. In the last four years I have done many projects with this company. Carol has long since left that job, yet, because I created many internal connections in the company, I have worked in all of its branches throughout the country. I continued to work with Carol in her last two jobs. Now she's preparing to start her own business, and she knows that I will be one of her biggest advocates, as she has been for me.

START YOUR THANK-YOU CHAIN

1. Think right now of all the connections you have within a company.

2. Go back and put into action the "Thank-You Chain" to touch base with some of these people.

3. Then, before you do anything else, go back to your database and enter the names of these people, your relationship to them, how you know them, and what business you may have gotten from them or have given them.

4. Watch the relationships in each of your accounts begin to multiply and see your network grow.

How many times have you lost business when your main contact has left the company? You have to start all over again to get the account! Better to have advocates throughout the organization who will champion your services.

Think of the companies you work for now and possible advocates you have developed. Remember to use your Thank-You Chain and be sure to show your appreciation for referrals others may give you. Keep this information in your database and stay in touch. Business can come from anyone on the other side of your door!

Your Friends and Neighbors

We work hard at building friendships that include mutual trust and respect. As you find out more about your friends' work, you'll want to help them, and over time, they will most likely want to help you with referrals.

Recently, my friend, Norma, experienced some challenging times in her business. She lost several key clients through circumstances that had nothing to do with her ability. I introduced Norma to another friend of mine who was looking for a top person in his company. Now Norma is working there happily and she has also become my advocate. I spoke at a meeting of one of her industry organizations, which resulted in three new projects for me. We both make sure we stay on each other's radar at all times.

Turning neighbors into advocates may take more time, but it will be worth the effort. Take the time to strike up conversations with people in your building or neighborhood. Often you"ll find that you have common interests.

My friend, Jan, struck up a conversation with a young man in her elevator and found out that he was a coin collector. She knew someone else whose hobby was coin collecting and arranged to have the young man attend a showing. His parents were so impressed with Jan's gesture that they invited her and her husband for cocktails at their home. During the evening, they discovered that they shared a lot of common interests. The young man's father is the managing partner at a large law firm and Jan is a publicist who works with law firms. Several months later, Jan has this firm as a client, along with another firm he referred to her. Like Jan, when you look at life with a "networking" awareness, your contacts will develop into something more.

You never know what can happen when you get to know your neighbors. It all starts with a genuine interest and curiosity about others, and using your self-marketing skills to create advocates. We meet people in a variety of ways, develop relationships, and then opportunities will present themselves—often when we least expect it.

Earning Referrals

While we cannot go around advertising ourselves, truly positive networking to build business is when we receive referrals from our clients, contacts, and friends. They believe in us so much that they want to send business our way.

Sometimes, they need a reminder—and that's why it's so important to stay on people's radar screens so you come to mind when they want someone with your expertise. When others take the time to refer us, it means they trust us, because we have earned that trust.

Here are some ways to earn trust and stay on your contacts' radar screens every day:

1. Get to know your clients as friends. Break bread with them, take them to an event, and develop a relationship with them as you would with a friend.

2. Provide service that dazzles your clients. Credibility is everything. Make it easy for them to brag about you, because you provide the top service and always go the extra mile.

3. Always think of them and what they need. Be proactive. Think of how you can make their life and work easier and more productive. Be the "go-to" person to fix things for them.

4. Give added value continually. Whatever you currently do for them, do some more and spice it up. Send them a note or a tip of the month (or week) to keep them informed about things they would want to know and information that could help their business.

5. Make connections for them. Help them find new business, a valuable connection, or anything that enhances their life or solves a problem.

6. Never keep score. Do it because you like and respect them. If you show that they're always on your radar screen, you'll find yourself on theirs as well.

Over time, you will earn their trust and respect and will see the results in a solid network of contacts that you can rely on and go to when you need help. From time to time, however, you may want to ask your clients and contacts for a "report card." Find an appropriate time to ask the following questions:

- What makes you do business with me?
- What could I be doing better?

- When you refer me to someone, what qualities about me come to mind?

Always remember that a referral is earned and is never given without thought and consideration.

Creating Rainmakers in Your Business

A rainmaker is someone who thinks about growing the business and finds ways to bring it in continually—someone who generates opportunities for new and current clients and thinks of ways to solve their problems. If everyone on your team did this, business would improve. To help everyone think like a business developer, you need to create awareness and communicate the idea to your team.

An accounting department manager at one company I work with trains her team to speak in "user-friendly" terms to customers. Rather than demanding payment, her team listens to the clients to understand their problems and finds ways to solve them. The team members have come to see how everything they do, from the way they speak to clients to the way they handle complaints, has a direct connection to the bottom line. While listening to a client's questions about a transaction, one staff member discovered both a concern and an opportunity for new business. She handled the concern, and relayed the conversation to staff members who were able to correct a problem that could have lost the business. They were then able to take advantage of an opportunity that created new business. This staff member in accounting now truly believes and understands that she is part of the rainmaking team.

Rainmaker: "a person (as in a law firm) who brings in new business; also: a person whose influence can initiate progress or ensure success." (*Merriam Webster's Collegiate Dictionary*)

Salespeople work hard to sell and create relationships with clients, but everyone in the company needs to build and maintain good relationships with clients. Everyone is in "sales." The operations manager, the marketing associate, and the IT technician represent the company every time they contact a client or a potential client. I like to say that we are all in sales, public relations, and customer service for the companies with which we work.

A dentist I know embraced the concept of rainmaking when she was losing patients because of the way her office staff treated them. In one case, a patient who left also took five family members, three people from her office, and two friends from her health club! My friend was fortunate to find out about this, as most people who receive poor treatment don't complain; they simply go away and then tell everyone about their experience. The dentist took immediate steps with her staff to correct the way they were handling patients and to stress the importance of their role in the practice. She was able to turn them into rainmakers.

People on your team need to know and understand a couple of ideas to think like business developers. And if your "team" is only you, then you'll have to work even harder and smarter because you are your business and you are your product. First, ask yourself what business you're in, whom you serve, what your clients' needs are, who your competitors are, what makes you different, and what unique benefits clients derive from your services. Second, ask what your mission statement is, and how it applies to your clients.

At one company I recently worked with, I asked the group to tell me their mission statement; only two out of forty people knew it, and most had no idea how it applied to them. It's your job to explain your mission and turn your employees into advocates. Look at your employee roster. How well do you know the employees who are in a position to relay your message? What can you do to incorporate some networking techniques into your day by going to a different area and spending a little time with each employee or department? I'm told Sam Walton, the late founder and CEO of Wal-Mart, not only knew the name of each of his employees, he also empowered them with a sense of ownership of their company. To this day, when I walk into a Wal-Mart, I'm greeted as a guest and treated as if I'm the only customer. The greeter at Wal-Mart is definitely a rainmaker. I'm also glad I own stock in the company!

Find ways to listen to your team and to hear their concerns and problems. It's important that you know how they interact with customers and that they understand how their relationship with customers affects the company. When people feel their work is important, they will become advocates for the company.

Give members of your team some appreciation; find ways to say thank you and to compliment them. Be sure to compliment them when they handle clients well or when they are advocates for your business. Studies show that people often work harder when they feel appreciated and that behavior that is rewarded is repeated. Instill in your people the power of networking—and how it is everyone's job. Reward them when they are successful at it. Lead by example.

SEVEN STEPS TO CLIENT RETENTION

1. Spend thirty minutes each day talking with two existing clients. Ask them what they want, what they need, what they like, and what they dislike. Ask them how they feel about the service they are currently receiving. Listen, implement changes, and suggest new ideas.

2. Invite your "champion clients" to serve on an advisory board.

3. Partner with your client in a workshop or special event. The more time you spend together, the more you bond.

4. Provide value every day. Offer something unique to show that you are creative, resourceful, and open to new ideas.

5. Find ways to connect on common ground, such as through hobbies, sports, special interests, religious affiliations, or school alumni groups.

6. Spend some time with your competitors and learn what they are doing. Find out from your clients what they hear in the outside world.

7. Conduct regular client formal or informal satisfaction surveys or interviews. These also provide valuable feedback.

Grow and Keep the Business You Have

It's much tougher to get new business than to grow, manage, and build the business you already have. What can your team do to grow existing business?

1. Make your relationship with your customer's job number one. Find ways to stay focused on the client. I know one firm that only calls at billing time. Needless to say, the client has found another firm—one that she feels is thinking of her all the time.

2. What do your clients need? What worries them? When you provide solutions, or at least show them that you care, you become a valuable addition to their team.

3. Who are your best customers, and why do they buy from you?

The principal objective of developing customers is to focus on the customers' needs. Happy customers are then cultivated as tremendous referral sources. Once you have a customer on your side, it's always easier to generate high-profit, word-of-mouth referrals. At the same time, your employees can be thinking beyond current ideas about what to do and how to help when they hear clients' concerns, problems, or situations (positive or negative). This affects everyone's job by contributing to the bottom line.

Customers want personal attention. In fact, we all do, and we are all someone's customer. See how you feel the next time someone you work with treats you well or not so well. You might consider assigning every customer someone whom they can call at any time, so at least there is always a "real person" to help. If that person is unable to handle the situation, he or she can direct the call to someone who can.

Your personal advocates can offer you the most valuable third-party endorsements. Think of them as part of your personal "buzz marketing" campaign. Therefore, be sure to take good care of the connections you have with them.

It's hard to believe that now it's time to wrap up everything we discussed so that you can build on what you've discovered to create a terrific "networking future."

Exercise: Who Are Your Advocates?

1. List ten contacts (clients, co-workers, employees, friends) who are advocates for you and your business.

2. How often are you in contact with each of them?

3. What is the biggest challenge each of them faces?

4. What associations or organizations do they belong to, and have you been to a meeting? Recently?

5. When did you last visit their Web site?

6. List at least one thing you could offer to do for them in the near future:

   - Write an article for a publication.
   - Offer to do a workshop pro bono.
   - Send an article of interest.
   - Give them a referral.
   - Make a useful introduction.
   - Help them solve a problem.
   - Send a card or note for a special occasion.

"See everything. Overlook a great deal. Improve a little."
—Pope John XXIII

"You and I can never do a kindness too soon, for we never know how soon it will be too late." **—Ralph Waldo Emerson**

CHAPTER 10

Today, Tomorrow and Your Future

> *"The best thing about the future is that it only comes one day at a time."*
> —**Abraham Lincoln**

Each day holds amazing networking opportunities for all of us. It truly is a small world, and you never know what will come from the connections or contacts you make. This is part of the fun of life, and I always hold on to that wonderful phrase, "If you want to make God laugh, tell him your plans." We just never know what's in store for us and how our lives can change or be enhanced, or how something entirely new can suddenly unfold. This can happen just because someone we've met makes a connection for us, we've reconnected with an old friend, or we've met someone through a chance encounter. Of course, much of this has to do with our following up. Things happen when we take that action step after life has presented us with a variety of opportunities.

This is my whole reason for writing this book. In business, which is such an integral part of our lives, the power of connection is the key. It's all about whom you know and who knows you. Often in my workshops and sessions I ask, "Is it always the smartest person who rises to the top?" Unanimously, people say, "No!" The truth is that being smart is your ticket in the door; but staying there, succeeding, and continuing to build your business, you also have to have great alliances and people skills—just what we've talked about throughout this book.

As soon as this chapter is finished and the book is done, a whole new group of stories and incidents will unfold that I could have written about. This only proves that each day offers us more experiences and opportunities.

One goal of this book was to keep its message concise and to the point. In today's crazy, time-starved world, people want information quickly and succinctly so they can act on it. I have always believed in less is more. Did you know that Abraham Lincoln's Gettysburg Address is 226 words long, and the Ten Commandments totals just 297 words? These are documents that get their points across succinctly. I've been kidded at times for my brevity, and I refer to myself as the "Cliff Notes Communicator." Today everything is so instant that, if I can give you some things to think about in a quick and efficient way, that's fine by me.

"WHEN YOU NEED A RELATIONSHIP, IT IS TOO LATE TO BUILD IT."

Live life with the state of mind that networking is everything.

Greet each day with a "networking eye and ear."

Learn and be aware.

To do this, live by these five steps:

1. Meet people and nurture your current network.

2. Listen and Learn from all the people you connect with.

3. Make connections for others.

4. Follow up.

5. Stay in touch.

This book is, and continues to be, a work in progress. New stories and "aha" moments happen every day. People like you call or e-mail me all the time to tell me of their success. Often they realize that they "have been networking all along and never realized it," or they tell me how they "have become more aware of this interesting phenomenon and state of mind." I especially enjoy when they tell me about their "best practices" and success stories, and how they have passed them down to their staffs, colleagues, and teams at work.

EVERYONE HAS A MOTHER...

Having just reconnected with a friend about a year ago, I established a business relationship with the association she heads. I met her second in command, Marshall, who, when not working for the association, also ran his own marketing company. Just recently, Marshall hired me to conduct a media-training program for one of his clients, a doctor.

As it turns out, I told the doctor during our session that his last name was uncommon and that I also knew a very nice woman with the same last name in the direct marketing industry, where I started my career. I asked him if he knew her. "Yes," he said, "she's my mother!"

Life is very funny. You never know where one connection may lead you to another.

Another time, sitting in a client's office, I was looking at his family picture and saw his wife. This was another great experience. I knew her from a company where I had done several projects. In business, however, she uses her maiden name. Who would have guessed that I would be in her husband's office? Again—you just never know. The world is truly connected.

We have been on quite a journey in this book. Very simply stated, we have gone through tips, strategies, and techniques for finding, growing, and keeping your business through the art and science of networking. The magic formula for all of this is in the doing of it. Start today with your awareness of it all and just remember these final, few facts.

Networking is truly a misunderstood word. Yes, there is some work involved, and when you implement what we've discussed in this book, you will see results over time and without keeping score. Just try to be aware of everything and live life with your networking eyes and ears open. Continually do your homework—always be prepared and organized and consistently apply the techniques we've discussed into your daily life.

Whenever I give a speech or a workshop, I always finish my program with what I call my Networking Acronym. It really condenses everything we've discussed in this book to its simplest form, and I hope you can take one thought, one idea, or one "aha'" moment from it and put it into action starting today. And, if you come up with some thoughts that I've left out, please e-mail or call me and let me know, and I will add them into my next speech, workshop, seminar, or book—and add you to my network!

N.E.T.W.O.R.K.I.N.G.

N—Remember people's Names. To each person his or her name is golden. On that same thought, continually Nurture the relationships of your current network.

E—Enthusiasm and Energy are key. Have the Empathy to understand that everyone has their own agenda; remember that Eye contact speaks volumes; and know when to Exit gracefully.

T—Talk less and listen more. Networking is about listening and learning from everyone you meet. It takes Time to develop Trust, and you always need to be in the mode of Thinking, "How can I help this person?"

W—Write. In this electronic age, a handwritten note or message stands out and will be remembered. There is some Work involved that you will have to incorporate into your daily life.

O—Organization is key. Keeping your contacts, records, and information is essential to your success. Remember, whenever you meet others, it is an Opportunity to learn from them and be a resource to help them. To do this, get into the habit of asking Open-ended, high-gain questions to develop rapport.

R—Research every event you attend. Know that the goal is to develop a Rapport that will lead to a Relationship of trust and Respect. Your Reputation is crucial, as you have built on it your whole life, so be careful when you Refer anyone, since that person is a Reflection on you.

K—Knowledge is power only when used. Much of this is common sense—it's just not common practice. Take the action steps to make things happen. Keep in touch and be creative about it. Also, I think every day about what my wonderful father said to me and continues to say as he smiles down from heaven: be Kind to people, give everyone you meet a smile and a handshake. My dad was the master of this and lives in my heart all the time.

I—Integrity is everything we have discussed. Your character and reputation are so important—remember that with integrity, nothing else matters, and without integrity, nothing else matters. To make your networking work, be sure to always take the Initiative. Waiting for someone else to make the first move is not the style of a proactive networker. Also, become Interested in other people and what you can learn from them.

N—Sometimes you have to say No—when you say yes to everyone, you say no to yourself; know your limits. On the other hand, when I hear "No," I often reverse the letters to "on" so that I am resourceful and creative in making and keeping my connections.

G—Set Goals for your networking achievements and remember to show Gratitude to those who help you. Also Give of your time and expertise to others. In the end, it's all about Going for it!

One Final Story—How Networking Has Changed My Life

I remember March 1993 very well. I had been working as a magazine publisher and was enjoying my work very much. Then, one day that March I received a phone call. It caused me to remember a promise that I had made to myself a few years earlier after I was in a bad car accident and had to be hospitalized.

I promised myself that I would start my own business. I didn't know how, but I did know that this was what I really wanted to do in life. In fact, I had been doing it all along. As a student of psychology and business, I've always enjoyed working with people and teaching business and life skills. I had already been speaking publicly through my work at Dale Carnegie, other associations, and for any opportunities that had popped up. I had also started teaching other workshops, yet I had not taken that leap of faith.

When that call came, it was from one of my publishing clients, Max, who was asking me to come and speak to his sales staff at their annual meeting. That morning, as I was preparing for my talk, I had a funny feeling that this experience might change my life. Fast forward to the next day. The presentation went very well, I thought.

Apparently, Max did as well. Afterward, he invited me in as a consultant and said, "We will be your first client," and for three years, two days a week, this company helped me lay the groundwork for my business. This gave me the opportunity to interact with a whole company of people—from the junior group who were just starting out and learning some of the rules of "business etiquette," to the senior people who needed to brush up on their presentation and pitching skills and wanted to learn how to work more effectively with their growing staffs.

As I met and worked with each person, I learned so much about each of them and practiced all of the techniques and strategies outlined in this book. The two hundred or so people with whom I worked there started another huge network in my life and business. People I had connected with left and went to other companies and brought me in to work with them and their teams (hence the beginning of my "Thank-You chain").

During the three years I worked at that company, Direct Media, I also worked diligently on figuring out what other industries I most wanted to work in. I practiced my 2-2-2 strategies, went to a lot of meetings and associations, met a lot of people, and then decided to join several organizations and become involved. More doors opened, and the very steps that we talked about in the "FIND" section of this book became, and still are, a devout practice of mine every day. I realized there was, and is, so much opportunity everywhere when you just take the time to live life with a networking eye and ear as I have learned to do—by offering to give first and be a resource to others.

After my accident, while I was lying in the emergency room of a local hospital in Massachusetts waiting to be airlifted to Boston's top hospital, I asked the doctors to call my parents so they would know what was happening. I still remember what my father, who was recuperating from open-heart surgery, said to me as they held the phone to my ear: "Keep fighting—you are my whole life."

Through the years, I have thought about what my dad said and how I promised myself that when I got well, I would go out, find a way to really make a real difference, and give back to all of the people who have helped me along the way. For me, being able to give back like this has been one of the most fulfilling parts of being alive. I now realize how this attitude and my dad's loving words are really what changed my life and made me want to be a "giver" as much as I possibly can. To me, that is what networking is really all about. The human relations principles that we discussed in this book are all practices we can use in our lives every day. You will see, or you have already seen, how everything we do is linked to others in our life—the way we touch them or the way they touch us— and how we influence them and they influence us.

As I look at my business and how it has grown, and continues to grow, I see that every single aspect of my life relates to finding, growing, and keeping lasting, powerful relationships. These have opened doors for me and created amazing opportunities. My hope is that you will close this book now and promise to act on some of the tips and ideas we have discussed, and then call or write me and let me know about all your wonderful successes.

Thank you for the opportunity to come into your life through this book, to share and discuss some of the interesting business strategies and lessons I have learned along the way from the many masters who have touched my life.

Exercise 1: What Do You Think Now?

Now that you've finished reading this book and doing the exercises, think about how your thoughts on networking might have changed. Please answer the following questions:

How has your definition of networking changed? How can you now create more business through your own power of networking? What are you going to do consistently?

_____

_____

_____

_____

_____

_____

List three new ideas about networking that you've learned.

1._____

2._____

3._____

Exercise 2: Know Yourself

Once you know effective networking techniques, you can use them in any situation. Wherever you network in business and in life, you need to remember the following:

Know who you are: Write down, in one or a few lines, how you want people to remember you. What would people say were your positive personality attributes?

_____

_____

_____

_____

_____

Focus on others: Write down your best conversation starters:

_____

_____

_____

_____

_____

Have a goal: Which goals are you most concerned with now in your business life?

❑ Getting a promotion   ❑ Political aspirations

❑ A career change   ❑ A lifestyle change

❑ A new business venture   ❑ Moving to a new location for work

❑ Clients for your business

What can you do today to start achieving your goals?

_____

_____

_____

_____

_____

Exercise 3: Do It Today

Which person will you contact today whom you haven't thought of before you did these exercises? Write that person's name down, how you will contact him or her, and what you want to accomplish.

_____

_____

_____

_____

_____

_____

The "Networking" Acronym—Fill in any other traits or techniques that come to mind. Take the next step and write next to each letter an experience that corresponds to that letter to make it real for you.

For example—"E," remember a time when you had a successful Exit strategy, or "W," where you started the process of Writing handwritten notes. Keep this going for yourself to maintain a networking tip log.

N _____

E _____

T _____

W _____

O _____

R _____

K _____

I _____

N _____

G _____

Exercise 4: Networking Action Plan

As a result of reading and working through this book, what are you going to do in the FIRST WEEK?

More of:

_____

_____

Less of:

_____

_____

Change:

_____

_____

By the END OF THE MONTH, I will:

Do more of:

_____

_____

Do less of:

_____

_____

Change:

_____

_____

In the NEXT THREE MONTHS, I will:

Do more of:

_____

_____

Do less of:

_____

_____

Change:

_____

_____

Remember, positive networking is all about giving more to others than you receive and always being a resource for them. Until we meet again, all the best in your networking!

1. Re-connect with four people a week. This week call a client or prospect you've been out of touch with, a former business colleague, a friend from the past and a current friend you haven't spoken with for awhile.

2. Make a list of key people in your industry or profession who—you would like to meet. Determine what organizations, places, and people they associate with and find ways to connect with them.

3. Join an organized networking group, go to the meetings, and find a way to become involved. Life is not a spectator sport.

4. Research and join an industry or professional group. Go to two meetings, meet two people, and set up two follow-up meetings before you make your decision to join. This is my "2-2-2 Strategy."

5. Join a civic group such as a Chamber of Commerce or a fundraising organization. Join for the sake of giving, not getting. You will get a lot back over time.

6. Follow your interests. Take a class, join a health club, or go on a different type of vacation. Remember, you need like-minded people in your network. Bonds will develop and create connections that you otherwise may not have made.

7. Volunteer, write an article, or join a committee in an organization. Take the action to become known in your organizations of choice. Results will happen.

Finding Personalized Gifts and Premiums

Coffee mugs, key chains, pens, magnets, and other useful items make great gifts that keep your name in front of your contacts. Finding sources for these can be a challenge because local phone books categorize them in so many different ways: advertising specialty items, corporate gifts, even trophies and awards. I recommend searching the Internet for "corporate gifts." Or, look at resource guides in trade publications.

Here are some tips for ordering personalized gift items:

- Ask for samples. Most companies will send you free samples of the products you are considering.

- Ask which items are available in small quantities. Prices for customized items are often quoted for large quantities. However, some are available in smaller quantities for a reasonable price. You just need to ask a sales representative.

- Ask to see a proof before your order is printed. See how the design looks and proofread the copy to avoid giving a gift with your name or company misspelled.

- Consider packaging. Some items like coffee mugs and pens need a box or a uniquely sized envelope for shipping purposes. Be sure to ask if the supplier offers packaging to make it easier for you to ship these items.

1. Give yourself permission to network. Changing your attitude to a positive one is the first step to networking success. Realize that networking is a state of mind and that it is pure people skills and connections.

   As you leave for work every day, give yourself a mental pep talk that you will make an effort to connect and reconnect with people. Also, set a goal for yourself each week. Do something as simple as saying hello to someone you don't know well or sending an email to a colleague in another department. This is the first step to achieving networking success in your business.

2. Make a list of "opening lines" to use when meeting someone new. Use open-ended questions that require more than a one-word answer, or at least follow up with an open-ended question.

   O—Open-ended questions are good, such as, "What brings you to this event?" or "What industry or side of the business are you in?"

   P—Practice some opening lines with friends and colleagues so you will all be prepared when you go to events.

   E—Engage the other person. Take your mind off of yourself and focus on finding out about the other person.

   N—Niceness is still key. A warm and approachable smile is always a great ice breaker and the start to your opening lines.

3. Develop a 30-second infomercial about yourself. Practice it until it becomes spontaneous and natural.

Ask yourself, "How do I want to be remembered?" and "What is the headline that will grab someone?" and "What is the benefit statement when I say what I do?" It is not about your job title—it is more important to get people to say, "Tell me more about what you do.."

4. Do your research before attending an event. Learn the basics about the organization and the people who will likely be there. Be prepared with your strategy and your tangible and intangible networking tool kits.

Your research is one of the most important habits to develop so that you have the competitive edge on every event you attend. You can find out about:

- the speaker
- the board of directors
- the organizer or president—that is why I always read their "letter" to readers
- any other member names that might be in their newsletter

Take the time to put together your own checklist for each event:

- Who is being honored or speaking?
- Who will be there—any chance of getting an advanced copy of attendees?
- Who do you already know who will be attending?
- What can you learn about them in advance?
- What is your goal for the event? To meet with a few people.

5. Develop your list of "get to know you" questions. These go deeper than "opening line" questions; they help you find out about the interests of the person you have just met.

This is how the rapport really starts to develop. Start asking and probing, instead of "grilling or drilling," by gently beginning the discussion so that you learn more. It is only when you have learned something about others and have conveyed a sincere interest that they will actually listen to you when you start talking again about what you do and how you do it.

My "get to know you questions" could be:

- How did you get involved in this industry or group?
- What books, movies, or plays have you seen recently?
- What do you like the most about your work and why?
- When you work with _____ (lawyers, bankers, consultants, etc), what do you look for that makes your job and life easier?
- What do you do when you're not at work—family, hobbies, special interests?
- If you could do any kind of work, what would it be, and what makes you say that?

My all-time favorite questions that give me a reason to follow up and stay in touch are:

- How do I know when I'm speaking to a potential client or a person you would like to meet?
- What is your preferred method of communication for staying in touch?

6. Keep a journal of "small talk" topics. These are about current events, industry topics, books, movies, community topics, and anything else you can think of. Start to keep that notebook and let it grow.

7. Set a goal for every event or meeting you attend. When you set a goal, you will really feel a sense of business accomplishment when you leave. The key is to actually do and accomplish something, so choose a goal that's right for you.

For example, I always set a goal that I will meet at least two new people. I will learn about them, their interests, their business, and how to follow up.

Here's something to help you remember:

G—Go up to at least two people with a goal in mind as you are speaking with them. Ask yourself, "Would I like to meet with them further, or is there a way I can help them?"

O—Observe people with both your eyes and ears. Also be sure to ask them open-ended questions so that you can learn more about them.

A—Attitude and Action steps are key to this tip. Be curious and eager to learn about some new people when you attend the meeting. It's important to take action instead of waiting for the other person to take the initiative.

L—Listen passionately to people. They will reveal their preferred means and style of communication.

8. Smile when meeting people, entering a room, or talking on the phone. A smile is the first step in building rapport. This goes for all of your internal meetings, sales calls, or customer events. Practice smiling at three new people every day.

9. Look the other person in the eye. Eye contact says you are focused on the conversation and are interested in what the other person is saying. The eyes are the windows of the soul and are considered a universal connection between people.

10. Listen with care. Concentrate on what the other person is saying instead of thinking about what you will say next. You will remember much more about the person and the conversation. Use the word LISTEN to help you:

   L—Look at the other person

   I—Involve yourself with nods to show you are listening

   S—Silence your mind

   T—Think of what the other person is saying

   E—Eye and Ear contact

   N—Note certain things about what is being said

11. Remember names by learning a system that works for you, and stick to it. Listen carefully when the name is said, repeat it frequently in conversation, and create a mind picture that will help you associate the person with the name.

12. Say something upbeat. Make a goal to look for positive attributes and give five compliments a day.

13. Once a month, have lunch with a friend, colleague, or client you have not seen for a while. Make a habit of face time.

14. Get out of your comfort zone at the next company function by sitting next to someone new, and then get to know him or her.

15. Use a script for making phone calls and practice it until the words flow naturally.

16. Begin with a compliment. It is a wonderful way to start a conversation when you may be at a loss as to how to break the ice. Everyone likes to hear a compliment.

17. When a conversation gets off track, use a "bridge" such as, "That reminds me of" to get back to the topic you had started.

18. Attend meetings and events with a specific purpose in mind. It could be just to meet the speaker or someone else you know will be there.

19. Set your own time limit. Give yourself permission to leave after a specific time when you have accomplished your goals, have connected with people, and have found a way to follow up with them.

20. When eye contact is difficult, look at the person's "third eye"—the spot just above the bridge of the nose between the eyes.

21. Network on the Internet. Online networking is an efficient way to establish some relationships with those in your field, especially if you or the other people are introverted.

22. Reward yourself for your networking success, whether it's for attending an event or landing new business as a result of a connection. You deserve it!

23. Pay attention to and appreciate all the opportunities that have developed due to your new and improved "networking awareness." Track one of them back every month, from its original seed to fruition.

1. Send three handwritten notes a day. Send these to people in your network to say, "thank you," to offer congratulations, to send an article of interest, to extend an invitation or just to say "thinking of you." Use any free time during the day to write these notes, and make them short and simple. Carry note cards and stamps with you.

2. Write an article or newsletter to send to your clients, prospects, and entire database. Make use of e-mail to stay on your clients' radar screen.

3. Send creative gifts as a thank you. Always remember people who have helped you and keep track of their special days. Develop and grow your list of reliable vendors with interesting gifts.

4. Keep your contacts in the loop by thanking them for referrals. Remember to build on your own "thank you" chain.

5. Make "face time" with your clients and contacts. Attend an event, play a sport, or have a meal or coffee together. Just do it.

6. Send cards for special events and birthdays. Buy a calendar just for networking opportunities and set it up using my monthly document system. Keep it up to date and continually add to it.

7. Every day, send an email to someone in your database whom you have been out of touch with just to say "hi" and "How are you."

8. Once a week, go though your contact list and call three people just to say "hello."

9. Find premiums or a "signature" premium to send to contacts to stay on their radar screen. Send something useful and functional—they will be appreciated.

10. Make the words "follow up" part of your daily mantra. Every day, follow up and follow through after any meeting, event, or get together.

11. Take action on what you promise. When you have told someone, "Let's do lunch sometime," make it happen. Pick up the phone and be proactive.

12. When you said you would send people something, be on time or even sooner to surprise and delight them. Just do it now and write a note to make sure it is done.

13. Give of your time and expertise generously. Be known as the "go to" person for your particular specialty. Remember to be a resource to others.

APPENDIX 4

Tips for Setting Up and Managing Your Contact Database

Develop a system to keep in touch with everyone in your network on a regular basis. As your list grows, divide it into categories and have a contact plan for each one. Quality versus quantity. Make sure you "touch" those closest to you often.

- Regularly review your contact list and "clean out" those contacts who, for whatever reason, are no longer in your life.

- Develop and maintain a database of your contacts. The system must work for you and you need to update it consistently.

- Be a collector and gather all sorts of information about your contacts, such as their interests, family, special dates, how you met, and the business connection.

- Find out the preferred method of communication for each contact and record it right away. Also, find out best time of day to reach them. Your contacts will appreciate it!

- Make and record notes about each meeting with someone and refer to your notes when communicating. This is easily done on your contact management system and can be linked to your handheld device for easy access when you're on the road.

- Develop your system for filing business cards depending on how you plan to use them in the future. Enter them into your database with special notes for follow-up.

- Within 24 hours, enter all information about contacts and meetings you have had. Tomorrow you will have more and they will pile up. Take action now.

APPENDIX 5

Tips for Managing Phone and E-mail Messages

Respond to phone and e-mail messages within 24 hours even when you are on the road. Technology has afforded us the ability to be totally "connected" in any situation. For business communications, you must follow up and follow through continually.

When you are going to be out of touch for a period, let people know with a message on your phone and an "away" message on your e-mail system. However, my motto is "out of sight, out of mind," so it's best to respond with a brief message, if you can. I like to avoid the "stress" of coming back to buckets of e-mail and voice mail messages.

Set aside a specific time (or times) in the day to read and answer e-mails. Use the "in-box" method:

1. Answer immediately all that you can. If I have to read a message later, I save it as "unread."

2. Forward those that can be handled by others.

3. Save newsletters and other reading material for later in the day.

4. Delete the rest.

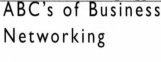

A—Action, Attitude

B—Belong to industry groups

C—Call your Contacts, Connect

D—Deliver what you say

E—Empathy and Eye Contact

F—Friendly approach

G—Set Goals— "Go for it," Gratitude, Give

H—Humor and Help go Hand in Hand

I—Be Interested and have Integrity

J—Join and get involved

K—Keep in touch and be Kind

L—Listen, Learn

M—Motivate yourself

N—Niceness pays

O—Ask Open-ended questions, Opportunity

P—Practice—be Professional

Q—Set a Quota

R—Be a Resource and do your Research

S—Strategy and Smile

T—Timing is everything—Trust is key

U—Understand others

V—Be Versatile

W—Write letters

X—Do it with love XO XO, or at least "like"

Y—Focus on "YOU" the other person

Z—Zoom with the possibilities of new and nurtured connections

Sample Notes

The "Thank You" Note

Purpose: Everyone loves to be appreciated. Send out sincere and concise notes to anyone who helps you, whatever the outcome is—even if nothing comes from it.

Text:

Dear Robert,

Thank you for taking the time to read over my manuscript and offering me some feedback. Although you decided not to publish it, I appreciated your input. It was great working with you. Perhaps there will be an opportunity in the future.

Sincerely,

Duane North

The "Nice Talking to (or Meeting) You" Note

Purpose: A meeting, whether by chance or intentional, is a great opportunity to strengthen your network. Make sure you follow up with your contacts by writing a quick note to let them know that you enjoyed speaking with them. This will open the door for further meetings and keep you in your contact's mind.

Text:

Dear Ruth,

I enjoyed sitting next to you at the accountants' convention last week. Your comment on the changing market for tax advisors got me thinking about new ways to expand my business. I really appreciated your ideas.

Best regards,

Ian Anderson

The "FYI" Note

Purpose: It is important to be a resource to others in your network. One great way to accomplish this is by sending them relevant articles, links to websites or pieces of information that are of interest to them.

Text:

Dear Tyler,

I remember that, at our lunch meeting, you mentioned your interest in Japanese cinema. I thought you might enjoy the enclosed article on Yasujiro Ozu's lost films. Perhaps you will find it informative.

Best regards,

Alisha Mann

The "Congratulations" Note

Purpose: There are few notes as fun to send or to receive as "congratulations" notes. Keep track of your contact's achievements, and make sure to be their cheerleader along the way. Over time, they will begin to associate you with their own successes.

Text:

Dear Andrew,

I heard about your promotion to vice president of sales. Congratulations! I was so glad to see that all your hard work really paid off. I'm sure that you'll do well in your new position.

Sincerely,

Laquisha Price

The "Thinking of You" Note

Purpose: It is important to stay on you contact's "radar screen." Sometimes, an effective way to do this is to just to let someone know that you are thinking of him or her.

Text:

Dear James,

I thought about you today when I opened the "Entrepreneurs" section of the paper. How is your business going? Were you able to find a good office assistant? I'd love to hear how you are doing, and be sure to let me know when you come through Atlanta again.

Best regards,

Thomas Sherman

Find! Grow! Keep! Business Development System©

The Nierenberg Group's Find! Grow! Keep! Business Development System© has a variety of workshops and keynote addresses that can be combined to provide the perfect training solution for your organization. Our most popular workshops are on the topic of networking, so I've included a couple sample programs here. Each program is customized for your team based on your objectives and on extensive pre-work that I do before each session.

Networking Workshop I: Creating Greater Business Relationships

Have you ever wondered how some people possess the type of marketing skills that make them shine and stand out in a crowd? They are able to walk into a room, create a presence, make connections, and persuade the client or prospect in a unique way.

What are the "secrets" of personal marketing and networking that cause the client to stand up and take note or to become engaged, whether at a social function, business meeting, or wherever?

In the global marketplace, everyone is seen as a commodity, and very often we find ourselves trying to catch up with our competition when it comes to marketing ourselves and our businesses. Yet many people do get the business because they have learned the tips, techniques, and strategies for selling and marketing themselves by letting people know who they are and what makes them and their company special. We are constantly marketing new ideas and products in our business. In this session, our whole focus will be on the opportunity to market the most important product all of us have—ourselves—and how to present and connect with our clients through networking and marketing skills. The main point is to create and win more business in a positive, relationship-building way.

Goals and Objectives:

- Provide an opportunity to sharpen personal marketing, communication, and networking skills
- How to "work the room" and adapt to your personality style
- Enhance your ability to meet, engage, and follow up with new and current clients
- Learn to "market" yourself, your company, your strengths, and your products
- How to network and connect, whether you're an Introvert or an Extrovert

Guarantee:

- You will walk away with a set of simple networking tools to put into action immediately
- You will learn to enhance your communication style to give you the competitive edge
- You will be armed with the ammunition to create more business with your new marketing know-how and action plan

The program is designed specifically for your company and according to your specific "wish list" and goals. All role plays, discussions, and scenarios will be from your real work life. We will critique on structure, style, delivery, and content. Then we will go over next steps and specify how each person did in connecting, engaging, probing, and strategy.

As in any program I develop, I send out a "pre-work" questionnaire to each participant via e-mail to serve as both an introduction and preparation for our time together. As an option, I will also call all of the people in advance if there are any questions or concerns. After the program, I send a follow-up report to each person. Also available, two months later, I will check in with them via email to see how they are doing with the skills they developed and respond to any questions or concerns they might have.

Here is what we cover:

- Welcome/Introduction/Goals/Objectives
- Short discussion on networking/personal marketing to win new business and retaining clients
- Personal marketing self-evaluation
- Why networking is important to developing new business
- How networking can be a misunderstood word and how to avoid networking pitfalls
- Networking techniques based on the 12-step process, from developing your opening lines- creating your 30 second self-introduction—to engaging and following up
- Idea generators and exit strategies when you're at a meeting or cocktail party
- The people in your current network
- People in your immediate, secondary, and universal network
- Building on your networking skills—the traits that fit according to your personality style
- Business building tactics to incorporate every day
- Tips and techniques for the quiet or introverted professional
- Expanding on your network

- Nurturing the network you develop
- Maintaining your database of wealth and information
- Your networking re-evaluation, action plan, and goals to move forward

The program is designed to be very interactive with exercises, discussions, and role-plays.

Networking Workshop II: For Seasoned Professionals

For the experienced business networker, the program is extremely discussion based. The session focuses on the following questions, which always lead to a lively interaction:

- After you make it to the top, why is it important to "stay connected"?
- What are your best networking and business development practices?
- How do you coach your staff and team on the importance of building alliances with external contacts and throughout different departments in your company?
- What do you personally do to stay connected?
- Tell us one amazing success story and how you have incorporated that into your business.
- Who is someone you admire as a great networker and business builder, and what is a positive quality that person possess?

At the end of the program, after having taken notes on everyone's input, we go around the room for a final time. People share one or two action items that they want to put into effect immediately or continue doing. I then send them follow-up reminders of their action items.

APPENDIX 9

Services and Programs Available from The Nierenberg Group, Inc.

Leading companies count on Andrea Nierenberg and her team for their training needs in sales, customer service, presentation and media training skills, networking, and motivation.

Personal Marketing/Networking

First Impressions—Find Lasting Business Relationships!

Your company's success improves when staff members become the "superstars" of your business. Everyone on your team can learn how to improve the image projected to prospects and clients through relationship marketing.

Customer Service

Keep Your Customers Happy and Your Business Growing!

Great customer service attracts customers and keeps them loyal. Your clients want what you want: genuine customer care that provides complete satisfaction.

Presentation Skills

Create Powerful and Memorable Presentations!

Improved presentation skills strengthen a company's image and enhance the appeal of its products and services. Regardless of experience, great presentations skills can be mastered. Videotaping and feedback are an integral part of the advanced program.

Motivational Techniques

Your Customers Stay Satisfied When Your Staff Is Motivated!

Encouraging self-motivation is the key for employees to achieve their highest potential. Inspiring each team member leads to better customer care and a more productive work environment.

Keynote Speeches

Imparting Your Organization's Vision and Goals

Andrea's keynotes are filled with practical, informative, and interactive material combined with her witty sense of humor. She jumpstarts any meeting, convention, or event.

Call or e-mail today to find out about how The Nierenberg Group, Inc. can help you and your organization.

212-980-0930 or info@mybusinessrelationships.com

INDEX

D

databases, contact, 197–205, 242
demeanor, 82
dependability, 7
dinner partners, 64–65
DISC® Personality Indicator System, 94
drinking, 123

E

EAGNY (The Executive's Association of Greater New York), 31–32
eating etiquette, 119, 123–126
e-cards, 189–190
effectiveness, networking, 90–91, 104–105, 132–133
e-mails
    e-cards, 189–190
    etiquette for, 127–129
    as follow-up, 157–158, 190–191
    management of messages, 243
    spam, 154–155
Emerson, Ralph Waldo, 80, 86
enthusiasm and energy, 223
etiquette
    arrival, 122
    business cards, 120, 122
    in conversation, 116–118, 122, 123
    drinking, 123
    eating, 119, 123
    e-mail, 127–129
    follow-up, 172
    handshakes, 123
    handwritten notes, 119
    introductions, 126–127

name dropping, 120
phone, 119, 129–130
referral requests, 120
stress and, 121
events
    goals for, 60–61
    industry, 27–29
    introductions to host, 61–62
    lines at, 62–63
    networking, 27
    non-networking, 130–131
ExecuNet, 30, 32
The Executive's Association of Greater New York (EAGNY), 31–32
exercises, ice breaking, 33, 34
exit strategies, 67–68, 168, 223
expertise sharing, 111–114, 196
extroverts, 138, 161–162
eye contact, 76–77, 87, 122, 149, 238

F

face time, 158–160, 194–196, 240
facial expressions, 81
family members, 18
feelers, 98–99
The Financial Executives Networking Group, 30
Financial Women's Association, 29
FIND Tips, 232
The Five O'Clock Club, 30, 32
focus (presence), 49, 82

J

job hunting, 32
Johnson, Dorothea, 81–82
jokes, 101

K

KEEP Tips, 240–241

L

ladder, networking, 25
Leads Club, 30
Le Tip International, Inc., 30
like-minded people, 14–15, 36
lines, getting into, 62–63, 69
listening
  acronym tips, 238
  to build trust, 74
  clarifying questions, 88
  effective skills in, 86–90
  gender differences and, 100, 101
  importance of, 49, 65, 223
  introverts and, 141–142

M

Make Me Feel Important About Me
  (MMFI-AM), 117
marketing, self-, 108–111
meals, business, 119, 123–126
meeting people. See also communication skills
  brainstorming exercises, 42–43
  event hosts, 61–62
  fear of, 44–45
  identifying target people, 47–48
  preparation, 46
  research for, 46–47
  self-permission, 46
  setting goals, 60–61

meetings
  chance, 19–20
  company, 32–34
  in-person, 158–160, 194–196, 240
  tag team sales, 162–163
mirrors, 51
Myers-Briggs Indicator, 94, 98–99

N

name dropping, 120
names, remembering, 77–79, 223, 238
name tags, 51, 122
National Association of Female
  Executives (NAFE), 30
negative networking, 47. See also etiquette
neighbors, 16
networking
  ABC's of, 244
  defined, 3
  effectiveness, 90–91, 104–105,
    132–133
  ladder, 25
  tool kits for, 49–52
Networking Acronym, 223–224
networking events and organizations,
  27–32
newsletters, 192
  The Nierenberg Group's Find!
  Keep! Business Development
  System©, 248–254
non-networking events, 130–131
Nonstop Networking (Nierenberg), 8,
  193–194, 207
nonverbal communications, 80, 88.
  See also body language

For more information on The Nierenberg Group and the *Find! Grow! Keep! Business Development System*©:

www.mybusinessrelationships.com

Also Check Out Our:

- Networking Self Test
- Streaming Video Presentations
- Free Downloadable Business Articles
- Networking Survey and Results
- Press & TV Coverage

And Sign Up For Our:

- Monthly E-mail Tips
- Quarterly E-mail Newsletter

All the Best In Your Networking Success!